W9-BMZ-299

French
Phrase Book
&
Dictionary

Berlitz Publishing
New York   Munich   Singapore

NO part of this book may be reproduced, stored in a retrieval system or transmitted in any form or means electronic, mechanical, photocopying, recording or otherwise, without prior written permission from APA Publications.

Contacting the Editors
Every effort has been made to provide accurate information in this publication, but changes are inevitable. The publisher cannot be responsible for any resulting loss, inconvenience or injury. We would appreciate it if readers would call our attention to any errors or outdated information. We also welcome your suggestions; if you come across a relevent expression not in our phrase book, please contact us: Berlitz Publishing, 193 Morris Avenue, Springfield, NJ 07081, USA. E-mail: comments@berlitzbooks.com

All Rights Reserved
© 2007 Berlitz Publishing/APA Publications GmbH & Co. Verlag KG, Singapore Branch, Singapore

Berlitz Trademark Reg. U.S. Patent Office and other countries. Marca Registrada. Used under license from Berlitz Investment Corporation.

Second Printing: November 2007
Printed in Singapore

Publishing Director: Sheryl Olinsky Borg
Senior Editor/Project Manager: Lorraine Sova
Editor: Claire Caro
Translation: Publication Services, Inc., Marie-Pierre Lassiva-Moulin
Cover Design: Claudia Petrilli
Interior Design: Derrick Lim, Juergen Bartz
Production Manager: Elizabeth Gaynor
Cover Photo: © Royalty-Free/Corbis
Interior Photos: p. 12 © Studio Fourteen/Brand X Pictures/AgeFotostock; p. 16 © Roger G. Howard; p. 17 © European Central Bank; p. 19 © Passport Stock/Fotosearch.com; p. 35 © Roman Krochuk, 2006/Shutterstock, Inc.; p. 39 © images-of-france/Alamy; p. 53 © Imageshop/Alamy; p. 51 © INSADCO Photography/Stocklib; p. 58 © Cole Group/Photodisc Green/Getty Images; p. 61 © Bananastock; p. 79 © Image Source/Alamy; p. 83 © Dianne Maire 2006/Shutterstock, Inc.; p. 88 © zimmytws, 2006/ Shutterstock, Inc.; p. 90 © Martin Child/Digital Vision/Getty Images; p. 102 © Imageshop/Alamy; p. 105 © Digital Vision/Getty Images; p. 110 © Bananastock; p. 116 © Medio Images/Fotosearch.com; p. 118 © WizData, Inc./Alamy; p. 122 © Benno de Wilde/Image Shop/AgeFotostock; p. 126 © PIXFOLIO/ Alamy; p. 138 © StockShot/Alamy; p. 142 © Illianski/Alamy; p. 144 © Jack Sullivan/Alamy; p. 147 © Christopher Robbins/Digital Vision/Getty Images; p. 149 © Royalty-Free/Corbis; p. 153 © David McKee, 2006/Shutterstock, Inc.; p. 154 © Iconotec/Fotosearch.com; p. 156 © Sébastien Baussais/Alamy; p. 164 © Andy Marshall/Alamy; p.176 © Andrew Bargery/Alamy

Contents

Survival

Food

People

Fun

Special Needs

Resources

Dictionary

Pronunciation

This section is designed to make you familiar with the sounds of French using our simplified phonetic transcription. You'll find the pronunciation of the French letters and sounds explained below, together with their "imitated" equivalents. This system is used throughout the phrase book; simply read the pronunciation as if it were English, noting any special rules below.

In French, all syllables are pronounced the same, with no extra stress on any particular syllable. The French language contains nasal vowels, which are indicated in the pronunciation by a vowel symbol followed by an N. This N should not be pronounced strongly, but it is there to show the nasal quality of the previous vowel. A nasal vowel is pronounced simultaneously through the mouth and the nose.

In French, the final consonants of words are not always pronounced. When a word ending in a consonant is followed with a word beginning with a vowel, the two words are often run together. The consonant is therefore pronounced as if it begins the following word.

Example	Pronunciation
comment	koh·mawN
Comment allez-vous?	koh·mawN tah·lay-voo

Consonants ———————————

Letter	Approximate Pronunciation	Symbol	Example	Pronunciation
cc	1. before e, i, like cc in accident	ks	**accessible**	ahk·seh·see·bluh
	2. elsewhere, like cc in accommodate	k	**d'accord**	dah·kohr
ch	like sh in shut	sh	**chercher**	shehr·shay
ç	like s in sit	s	**ça**	sah

Letter	Approximate Pronunciation	Symbol	Example	Pronunciation
g	1. before e, i, y, like s in pleasure	zh	**manger**	mawN·zhay
	2. before a, o, u, like g in go	g	**garçon**	gahr·sohN
h	always silent		**homme**	ohm
j	like s in pleasure	zh	**jamais**	zhah·may
qu	like k in kill	k	**qui**	kee
r	rolled in the back of the mouth, like gargling	r	**rouge**	roozh
w	usually like v in voice	v	**wagon**	vah·gohN

B, c, d, f, k, l, m, n, p, s, t, v, x and z are pronounced as in English.

Vowels

Letter	Approximate Pronunciation	Symbol	Example	Pronunciation
a, à, â	between the a in hat and the a in father	ah	**mari**	mah·ree
e	sometimes like a in about	uh	**je**	zhuh
è, ê, e	like e in get	eh	**même**	mehm
é, ez	like a in late	ay	**été**	ay·tay
i	like ee in meet	ee	**il**	eel
o, ô	generally like o in roll	oh	**donner**	doh·nay
u	like ew in dew	ew	**une**	ewn

Sounds spelled with two or more letters

Letter	Approximate Pronunciation	Symbol	Example	Pronunciation
ai, ay, aient, ais, ait, aî, ei	like a in late	ay	j'ai vais	zhay vay
ai, ay, aient, ais, ait, aî, ei	like e in get	eh	chaîne peine	shehn pehn
(e)au	similar to o	oh	chaud	shoh
eu, eû, œu	like u in fur but short like a puff of air	uh	euro	uh·roh
euil, euille	like uh + y	uhy	feuille	fuhy
ail, aille	like ie in tie	ie	taille	tie
ille	1. like yu in yucca	eeyuh	famille	fah-meeyuh
	2. like eel	eel	ville	veel
oi, oy	like w followed by the a in hat	wah	moi	mwah
ou, oû	like o in move or oo in hoot	oo	nouveau	noo·voh
ui	approximately like wee in between	wee	traduire	trah·dweer

There are approximately 129 million French speakers worldwide. French is an official language in 30 countries and the United Nations. French is spoken by 4 million people in Belgium, 7 million in Canada, 60.5 million in France and 1.3 million in Switzerland. It is also an official language of 22 African nations.

How to Use This Book

These essential phrases can also be heard on the audio CD.

Sometimes you see two alternatives in italics, separated by a slash. Choose the one that's right for your situation.

Essential

I'm on *vacation [holiday]/business*.	**Je suis en *vacances/voyage d'affaires*.** zhuh swee zawN *vah·kawNs/ vwah·yahzh dah·fehr*
I'm going to…	**Je vais *à/aux*…** zhuh vay *ah/oh*…
I'm staying at the…Hotel.	**Je reste à l'hôtel…** zhuh rehst ah loh·tehl…

You May See…

DOUANES	Words you may see are shown in *You May See* boxes.	customs
ARTICLES HORS TAXES		duty-free goods
PRODUITS À DÉCLARER		goods to declare

Ticketing

A…ticket.	**Un billet pour…** uhN bee·yay poor…
– one-way	**– un aller simple** uhN nah·lay sehN·pluh
– round-trip [return]	**– un aller-retour** uhN nah·lay·ruh·toor
– first class	**– première classe** pruh·meeyehr klahs
– business class	**– classe affaire** klah sah·fehr
– economy class	**– classe économique** klah say·koh·noh·meek

Any of the words or phrases preceded by dashes can be plugged into the sentence above.

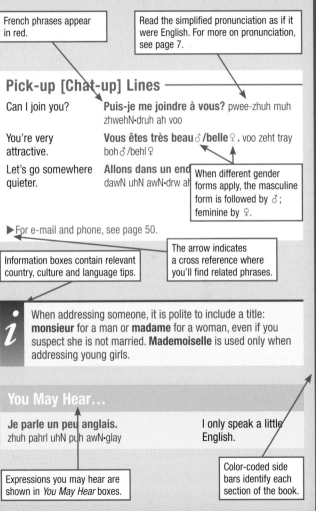

French phrases appear in red.

Read the simplified pronunciation as if it were English. For more on pronunciation, see page 7.

Pick-up [Chat-up] Lines

Can I join you?   **Puis-je me joindre à vous?** pwee-zhuh muh zhwehN·druh ah voo

You're very attractive.   **Vous êtes très beau**♂**/belle**♀**.** voo zeht tray boh♂/behl♀

Let's go somewhere quieter.   **Allons dans un end** dawN uhN awN·drw a

When different gender forms apply, the masculine form is followed by ♂; feminine by ♀.

▶ For e-mail and phone, see page 50.

The arrow indicates a cross reference where you'll find related phrases.

Information boxes contain relevant country, culture and language tips.

i When addressing someone, it is polite to include a title: **monsieur** for a man or **madame** for a woman, even if you suspect she is not married. **Mademoiselle** is used only when addressing young girls.

You May Hear...

Je parle un peu anglais. zhuh pahrl uhN puh awN·glay

I only speak a little English.

Expressions you may hear are shown in *You May Hear* boxes.

Color-coded side bars identify each section of the book.

▼ *Survival*

Arrival and Departure

Essential

I'm on *vacation [holiday]*/business.

Je suis en *vacances/voyage d'affaires.* zhuh swee zawN *vah·kawNs/vwah·yahzh dah·fehr*

I'm going to…

Je vais *à/aux…* zhuh vay *ah/oh…*

I'm staying at the…Hotel.

Je reste à l'hôtel… zhuh rehst ah loh·tehl…

▶For when to use **à** or **aux**, see page 173.

You May Hear…

Votre passeport, s'il vous plaît. voh·truh pahs·pohr seel voo play

Your passport, please.

Quel est le but de votre visite? keh lay luh bewt duh voh·truh vee·zeet

What's the purpose of your visit?

Où restez-vous? oo rehs·tay·voo

Where are you staying?

Combien de temps restez-vous? kohN·beeyehN duh tawN rehs·tay·voo

How long are you staying?

Avec qui êtes-vous? ah·vehk kee eht·voo

Who are you here with?

Passport Control and Customs

I'm just passing through.

Je suis juste en transit. zhuh swee zhews tawN trawN·zeet

I'd like to declare…

Je voudrais déclarer… zhuh voo·dray day·klah·ray…

I have nothing to declare.

Je n'ai rien à déclarer. zhuh nay reeyehN nah day·klah·ray

You May Hear...

Rien à déclarer? reeyehN nah day·klah·ray

Anything to declare?

Vous devez payer la taxe sur ceci.
voo duh·vay pay·yay lah tahks sewr suh·see

You must pay duty on this.

Ouvrez ce sac. oo·vray suh sahk

Open this bag.

You May See...

DOUANES	customs
ARTICLES HORS TAXES	duty-free goods
PRODUITS À DÉCLARER	goods to declare
RIEN À DÉCLARER	nothing to declare
CONTRÔLE DE PASSEPORT	passport control
POLICE	police

Money and Banking

Essential

Where's...?

Où est...? oo ay...

– the ATM

– **le distributeur automatique de billets** luh dee·stree·bew·tuhr oh·toh·mah·teek duh bee·yay

– the bank

– **la banque** lah bawNk

– the currency exchange office

– **le bureau de change** luh bew·roh duh shawNzh

When does the bank *open/close*?	**Quand est-ce que la banque *ouvre/ferme*?** kawN ehs kuh lah bawNk oo·vruh/fehrm
I'd like to change *dollars/pounds* into euros.	**Je voudrais échanger des *dollars/livres sterling* en euros.** zhuh voo·dray ay·shawN·zhay day *doh·lahr/lee·vruh stayr·leeng* awN nuh·roh
I'd like to cash traveler's checks [cheques].	**Je voudrais encaisser des chèques de voyages.** zhuh voo·dray awN·kay·say day shehk duh vwah·yahzh

ATM, Bank and Currency Exchange

I'd like to *change money/get a cash advance*.	**Je voudrais *changer de l'argent/obtenir une avance en liquide*.** zhuh voo·dray *shawN·zhay duh lahr·zhawN/ohb·tuh·neer ewn ah·vawNs awN lee·keed*
What's the exchange *rate/fee*?	**Quel est le *taux de/prix du* change?** keh lay luh *toh duh/pree dew* shawNzh
I think there's a mistake.	**Je pense qu'il y a une erreur.** zhuh pawNs keel·yah ewn ay·ruhr
I lost my traveler's checks [cheques].	**J'ai perdu mes chèques de voyages.** zhay pehr·dew may shehk duh vwah·yahzh
My card...	**Ma carte...** mah kahrt...
– was lost	**– a été perdue** ah ay·tay pehr·dew
– was stolen	**– a été volée** ah ay·tay voh·lay
– doesn't work	**– ne fonctionne pas** nuh fohNk·seeyohn pah
The ATM ate my card.	**Le distributeur automatique de billets a avalé ma carte.** luh dee·stree·bew·tuhr oh·toh·mah·teek duh bee·yay ah ah·vah·lay mah kahrt

▶ For numbers, see page 173.

i At some banks, cash can be obtained from ATMs with Visa™, Eurocard™, American Express® and many other international cards. Instructions are often given in English. Banks with a **Change** sign will exchange foreign currency. You can also change money at travel agencies and hotels, but the rate will not be as good. Remember to bring your passport when you want to change money.

You May See...

INSÉREZ LA CARTE ICI	insert card here
ANNULER	cancel
EFFACER	clear
VALIDER	enter
CODE SECRET	PIN
RETRAIT	withdrawal
DU COMPTE COURANT	from checking [current account]
DU COMPTE ÉPARGNE	from savings
REÇU	receipt

You May See...

The French currency is the **euro**, **€**, which is divided into 100 **cents**.

Coins: 1, 2, 5, 10, 20 and 50 **cents**; €1, 2

Bills: **€**5, 10, 20, 50, 100, 200 and 500

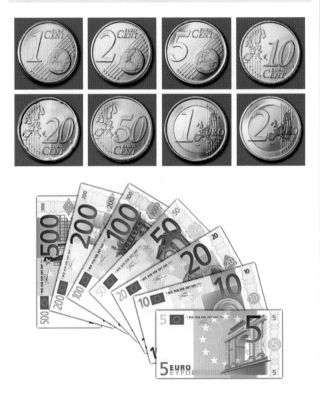

Transportation

Essential

How do I get to town?	**Comment vais-je en ville?** koh·mawN vay·zhuh awN veel
Where's…?	**Où est…?** oo ay…
– the airport	**– l'aéroport** lah·ay·roh·pohr
– the train [railway] station	**– la gare** lah gahr
– the bus station	**– la gare routière** lah gahr roo·tee·yehr
– the subway [underground] station	**– le métro** luh may·troh
Is it far from here?	**C'est loin d'ici?** say lwehN dee·see
Where do I buy a ticket?	**Où puis-je acheter un billet?** oo pwee·zhuh ah·shtay uhN bee·yay
A *one-way/round-trip* [return] ticket to…	**Un billet *aller simple/aller-retour*…** uhN bee·yay *ah·lay sehN·pluh/ah·lay·ruh·toor*…
How much?	**Combien ça coûte?** kohN·beeyehN sah koot
Which *gate/line*?	**Quelle *porte/ligne*?** kehl *pohrt/lee·nyuh*
Which platform?	**Quel quai?** kehl kay
Where can I get a taxi?	**Où puis-je prendre un taxi?** oo pwee·zhuh prawN·druh uhN tahk·see
Take me to this address.	**Conduisez-moi à cette adresse.** kohN·dwee·zay·mwah ah seh tah·drehs
Can I have a map?	**Puis-je avoir une carte?** pwee·zhuh ah·vwahr ewn kahrt

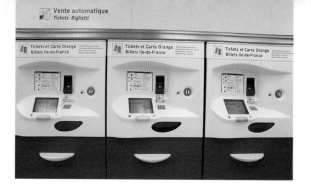

Ticketing

When's…to Paris?	**Quand est…pour Paris?** kawN tay…poor pah·ree
– the (first) bus	– **le (premier) bus** luh (pruh·meeyay) bews
– the (next) flight	– **le (prochain) vol** luh (proh·shehN) vohl
– the (last) train	– **le (dernier) train** luh (dehr·neeyay) trehN
Where do I buy a ticket?	**Où puis-je acheter un billet?** oo pwee·zhuh ah·shtay uhN bee·yay
One/Two ticket(s), please.	***Un/Deux* billet(s), s'il vous plaît.** uhN/duh bee·yay seel voo play
For *today/tomorrow*.	**Pour *aujourd'hui/demain*.** poor oh·zhoor·dwee/duh·mehN

▶For days, see page 176.
▶For time, see page 175.

A...ticket.	**Un billet pour...** uhN bee·yay poor...
– one-way	**– un aller simple** uhN nah·lay sehN·pluh
– round-trip [return]	**– un aller-retour** uhN nah·lay·ruh·toor
– first class	**– première classe** pruh·meeyehr klahs
– business class	**– classe affaire** klah sah·fehr
– economy class	**– classe économique** klah say·koh·noh·meek
How much?	**Combien ça coûte?** kohN·beeyehN sah koot
Is there a discount for...?	**Y-a-t-il une réduction pour...?** yah·teel ewn ray·dewk·see·yohN poor...
– children	**– les enfants** lay zawN·fawN
– students	**– les étudiants** lay zay·tew·dee·yawN
– senior citizens	**– les seniors** lay say·nyohr
– tourists	**– les touristes** lay too·reehst
The *express bus/ express train*, please.	*Le bus direct/L'express*, **s'il vous plaît.** luh bews dee·rehkt/lehk·sprehs seel voo play
The local *bus/train*, please.	**Le** *bus/train* **régional, s'il vous plaît.** luh *bews/trehN* ray·zheeyoh·nahl seel voo play
I have an e-ticket.	**J'ai un billet électronique.** zhay uhN bee·yay ay·lehk·troh·neek
Can I buy a ticket on the *bus/train*?	**Puis-je acheter un billet dans le** *bus/ train*? pwee·zhuh ah·shtay uhN bee·yay dawN luh *bews/trehN*
Do I have to stamp the ticket before boarding?	**Dois-je composter mon billet avant de monter?** dwah·zhuh kohN·poh·stay mohN bee·yay ah·vawN duh mohN·tay
How long is this ticket valid?	**Jusqu'à quand le billet est-il valable?** zhew·skah kawN luh bee·yay eh·teel vah·lah·bluh

Can I return on the same ticket?	**Puis-je utiliser le même billet pour le retour?** pwee·zhuh ew·tee·lee·zay luh mehm bee·yay poor luh rhuh·toor
I'd like to… my reservation.	**Je voudrais…ma réservation.** zhuh voo·dray…mah ray·zehr·vah·seeyohN
– cancel	**– annuler** ah·new·lay
– change	**– échanger** ay·shawN·zhay
– confirm	**– confirmer** kohN·feer·may

Plane

Getting to the Airport

How much is a taxi to the airport?	**Combien coûte le trajet en taxi jusqu'à l'aéroport?** kohN·beeyehN koot luh trah·zhay awN tahk·see zhew·skah lah·ay·roh·pohr
To…Airport, please.	**À l'aéroport de…, s'il vous plaît.** ah lah·ay·roh·pohr duh…seel voo play
My airline is…	**Ma compagnie aérienne est…** mah kohN·pah·nee ah·ay·ree·yeh nay…
My flight leaves at…	**Mon vol part à…** mohN vohl pahr ah…
I'm in a rush.	**Je suis pressé ♂/pressée ♀.** zhuh swee preh·say
Can you take an alternate route?	**Pouvez-vous prendre une route différente?** poo·vay·voo prawN·druh ewn root dee·fay·rawNt
Can you drive *faster/slower*?	**Pouvez-vous conduire *plus/moins* vite?** poo·vay·voo kohN·dweer *plew/mwehN* veet

i France has more than 20 main airports. Paris's two airports are **Roissy-Charles de Gaulle**, located 15 miles (23 km) north of the city, and **Orly**, located 9 miles (14 km) south of the city. **Air France** is France's principal domestic airline, with services between major cities: Paris, Lille, Lyon, Strasbourg, Grenoble, Bordeaux, Clermond-Ferrand, Nantes, Marseilles, Nice, Toulouse and more.

You May Hear...

Quelle compagnie aérienne prenez-vous? kehl kohN·pah·nee ah·ay·ree·yehn pruh·nay·voo	What airline are you flying?
Nationale ou internationale? nah·seeyoh·nahl oo ehN·tehr·nah·seeyoh·nahl	Domestic or international?
Quel terminal? kehl tehr·mee·nahl	What terminal?

You May See...

LES ARRIVÉES	arrivals
LES DÉPARTS	departures
RETRAIT DES BAGAGES	baggage claim
SÉCURITÉ	security
VOLS NATIONAUX	domestic flights
VOLS INTERNATIONAUX	international flights
ENREGISTREMENT	check-in
ENREGISTREMENT ÉLECTRONIQUE	e-ticket check-in
PORTES DE DÉPART	departure gates

Check-In and Boarding

Where's check-in?	**Où est l'enregistrement?** oo ay lawN·ruh·zhees·truh·mawN
My name is…	**Je m'appelle…** zhuh mah·pehl…
I'm going to…	**Je vais à…** zhuh vay ah…
I have…	**J'ai…** zhay…
– one suitcase	**– une valise** ewn vah·leez
– two suitcases	**– deux valises** duh vah·leez
– one carry-on [piece of hand luggage]	**– un bagage à main** uhN bah·gahzh ah mehN
How much luggage is allowed?	**Combien de bagages sont permis?** kohN·beeyehN duh bah·gahzh sohN pehr·mee
Is that pounds or kilos?	**Est-ce que ce sont des livres ou des kilos?** ehs kuh suh sohN day leevr oo day kee·loh
Which terminal?	**Quel terminal?** kehl tehr·mee·nahl
Which gate?	**Quelle porte?** kehl pohrt
I'd like *a window/ an aisle* seat.	**Je voudrais un siège *hublot/couloir.*** zhuh voo·dray uhN see·yehzh *ew·bloh/kool·wahr*
When do we *leave/arrive*?	**Quand est-ce que nous *partons/ arrivons*?** kawN tehs kuh noo *pahr·tohN/ zah·ree·vohN*
Is the flight delayed?	**Est-ce que le vol est retardé?** ehs kuh luh vohl ay ruh·tahr·day
How late?	**Combien de retard a-t-il?** kohN·beeyehN duh ruh·tahr ah·teel

You May Hear…

Au suivant! oh swee·vawN

Next!

Votre *passeport/billet*, s'il vous plaît.
voh·truh *pahs·pohr/bee·yay* seel voo play

Your *passport/ticket*, please.

Avez-vous des bagages à enregistrer?
ah·vay·voo day bah·gahzh ah awN·ruh·zhees·tray

Are you checking any luggage?

C'est trop gros pour un bagage à main.
say troh groh poor uhN bah·gahzh ah mehN

That's too large for a carry-on [piece of hand luggage].

Avez-vous fait ces bagages vous-même?
ah·vay·voo feh seh bah·gahzh voo·mehm

Did you pack these bags yourself?

Est-ce que quelqu'un vous a donné quelque chose à porter? ehs kuh kehl·kuhN voo zah doh·nay kehl·kuh shoh zah pohr·tay

Did anyone give you anything to carry?

Retirer vos chaussures.
ruh·tee·ray voh shoh·sewr

Take off your shoes.

Embarquement immédiat…
awN·bahr·kuh·mawN ee·meh·dyah…

Now boarding…

Luggage

Where *is/are*…?   **Où *est/sont*…?** oo *ay/sohN*…

– the luggage carts [trolleys]   **– les chariots** lay shah·ree·yoh

– the luggage lockers   **– les consignes** lay kohN·see·nyuh

– the baggage claim   **– le retrait des bagages** luh ruh·tray day bah·gahzh

My luggage has been *lost/stolen*.   **Mon bagage a été *perdu/volé*.** mohN bah·gahzh ah ay·tay *pehr·dew/voh·lay*

My suitcase is damaged.   **Ma valise est endommagée.** mah vah·leez ay awN·doh·mah·zhay

Finding Your Way

Where *is/are*…?	**Où *est/sont*…?** oo *ay/sohN*…
– the currency exchange	– **le bureau de change** luh bew·roh duh shawNzh
– the car rental [hire]	– **l'agence de voitures de location** lah·zhawNs duh vwah·tewr duh loh·kah·seeyohN
– the exit	– **la sortie** lah sohr·tee
– the taxis	– **les taxis** lay tahk·see
Is there… into town?	**Est-ce qu'il y a…pour aller en ville?** ehs keel·yah…poor ah·lay awN veel
– a bus	– **un bus** uhN bews
– a train	– **un train** uhN trehN
– a subway [underground]	– **un métro** uhN may·troh

▶ For directions, see page 34.

Train

Where's the train [railway] station?	**Où est la gare?** oo ay lah gahr
How far is it?	**C'est loin d'ici?** say lwehN dee·see
Where *is/are*…?	**Où *est/sont*…?** oo *ay/sohN*…
– the ticket office	– **le bureau de vente des billets** luh bew·roh duh vawNt day bee·yay
– the information desk	– **le bureau de renseignements** luh bew·roh duh rawN·seh·nyuh·mawN
– the luggage lockers	– **les consignes** lay kohN·see·nyuh
– the platforms	– **les quais** lay kay

▶ For directions, see page 34.

▶ For ticketing, see page 19.

You May See...

QUAIS	platforms
INFORMATION	information
RÉSERVATIONS	reservations
SALLE D'ATTENTE	waiting room
ARRIVÉES	arrivals
DÉPARTS	departures

Questions

Can I have a schedule [timetable]?	**Puis-je avoir les horaires?** pwee•zhuh ah•vwahr lay zhoh•rehr
How long is the trip?	**Combien de temps dure le voyage?** kohN•beeyehN duh tawN dewr luh vwah•yahzh
Is it a direct train?	**Est-ce que c'est un train direct?** ehs kuh say tuhN trehN dee•rehkt
Do I have to change trains?	**Est-ce que je dois changer de train?** ehs kuh zhuh dwah shawN•zhay duh trehN
Is the train on time?	**Est-ce que le train est à l'heure?** ehs kuh luh trehN ay ah luhr

i France has a fast and efficient train network operated by **SNCF** (**Société Nationale des Chemins de Fer**). The **SNCF** links over 50 cities in France, with the central hub in Paris. Paris has six train stations that service the rest of France and Europe. The **TGV** (**Train à Grande Vitesse**) is an extra-high-speed train that runs routes from Paris to Bordeaux, Brest, La Rochelle, Lille, Calais, Lyon and Marseilles. It is expensive and advance reservations are required.

The **Eurostar** offers fast and frequent service from London (Waterloo International) or Ashford stations to Paris. The **Eurotunnel** provides car travel from Folkestone, U.K., to Calais, France.

Departures

Which track
[platform] to…?

Quel quai pour…? kehl kay poor…

Is this the *track
[platform]/
train* to…?

Est-ce que c'est le *quai/train* pour…?
ehs kuh say luh *kay/trehN* poor…

Where is track
[platform]…?

Où est le quai…? oo ay luh kay…

Where do I
change for…?

Où dois-je changer pour…?
oo dwah·zhuh shawN·zhay poor…

Boarding

Can I *sit here/open
the window*?

Puis-je *m'asseoir ici/ouvrir la fenêtre*?
pwee·zhuh *mah·swahr ee·see/oo·vreer lah
fuh·neh·truh*

That's my seat.

C'est ma place. say mah plahs

Here's my
reservation.

Voici ma réservation. vwah·see mah
ray·sehr·vah·seeyohN

You May Hear…

Billets, s'il vous plaît.
bee·yay seel voo play

Tickets, please.

Vous devez changer à…
voo duh·vay shawN·zhay ah…

You have to change
at…

Prochain arrêt…
proh·shehN nah·reh…

Next stop…

Bus

Where's the bus station?	**Où est la station de bus?** oo ay lah stah·seeyohN duh bews
How far is it?	**C'est loin d'ici?** say lwehN dee·see
How do I get to…?	**Comment vais-je à…?** koh·mawN vay·zhuh ah…
Is this the bus to…?	**Est-ce le bus pour…?** ehs luh bews poor…
Can you tell me when to get off?	**Pouvez-vous me dire quand je dois descendre?** poo·vay·voo muh deer kawN zhuh dwah deh·sawN·druh
Do I have to change buses?	**Est-ce que je dois changer de bus?** ehs kuh zhuh dwah shawN·zhay duh bews
Stop here, please!	**Arrêtez-vous ici, s'il vous plaît!** ah·ray·tay·voo ee·see seel voo play

▶ For ticketing, see page 19.

i Bus tickets can be purchased from the bus driver, or you can buy them in subway stations or at tobacconists. Tickets purchased for the subway can also be used for the bus system. Remember to validate your ticket in the machine when boarding the bus.

You May See…

ARRÊT DE BUS	bus stop
DEMANDER L'ARRÊT	request stop
ENTRÉE/SORTIE	entrance/exit
COMPOSTER VOTRE BILLET	stamp your ticket

Subway [Underground]

Where's the subway [underground] station?	**Où est la station de métro?** oo ay lah stah·seeyohN duh may·troh
A map, please.	**Une carte, s'il vous plaît.** ewn kahrt seel voo play
Which line for…?	**Quelle est la ligne pour…?** keh lay lah lee·nyuh poor…
Which direction?	**Quelle direction?** kehl dee·rayk·seeyohN
Do I have to transfer [change]?	**Est-ce que je dois changer de ligne?** ehs kuh zhuh dwah shawN·zhay duh lee·nyuh
Is this the subway [train] to…?	**Est-ce que c'est le métro pour…?** ehs kuh say luh may·troh poor…
How many stops to…?	**Combien d'arrêts jusqu'à…?** kohN·beeyehN dah·ray zhew·skah…
Where are we?	**Où sommes-nous?** oo suhm·noo

▶ For ticketing, see page 19.

Many of France's major cities have **métro** (subway) systems, including Paris, Lille, Toulouse, Lyon, Marseilles, Rennes and Rouen. The **métro** systems are well marked with easy-to-read maps available at the stations. Most systems run from approximately 5:00 a.m. until 12:00 a.m., with some running slightly shorter or longer hours. In most cities, the same tickets work for the bus, **métro** and tram systems. Some cities require a ticket for each leg of the journey, while others allow you to travel the entire network on one ticket. Tickets can usually be purchased at the station or at tobacconists and other retailers.

Boat and Ferry

When is the ferry to…?	**Quand part le ferry pour…?** kawN pahr luh fay·ree poor…
Can I take my car?	**Est-ce que je peux prendre ma voiture?** ehs kuh zhuh puh prawN·druh mah vwah·tewr

▶ For ticketing, see page 19.

You May See...

CANOTS DE SAUVETAGE	life boats
GILET DE SAUVETAGE	life jacket

i Ferry service is available to and from the U.K., the Republic of Ireland and the Channel Islands to the north of France. Ferries carry cars as well as passengers. Services can be booked through the individual ferry companies or through a travel agent.

Bicycle and Motorcycle

I'd like to rent [hire]…	**Je voudrais louer…** zhuh voo·dray looway…
– a bicycle	– **une bicyclette** ewn bee·see·kleht
– a moped	– **une mobylette** ewn moh·bee·leht
– a motorcycle	– **une moto** ewn moh·toh
How much per *day/week*?	**Combien par *jour/semaine*?** kohN·beeyehN pahr *zhoor/suh·mehn*
Can I have a *helmet/lock*?	**Puis-je avoir un *casque/cadenas*?** pwee·zhuh ah·vwahr uhN *kas·kuh/kah·duh·nah*

Taxi

Where can I get a taxi?	**Où puis-je prendre un taxi?** oo pwee·zhuh prawN·druh uhN tahk·see
Do you have the number for a taxi?	**Avez-vous le numéro d'un taxi?** ah·vay·voo luh new·may·roh duhN tahk·see
I'd like a taxi *now/ for tomorrow at…*	**Je voudrais un taxi *maintenant/pour demain à…*** zhuh voo·dray uhN tahk·see mehN·tuh·nawN/poor duh·mehN nah…
Pick me up at…	**Prenez-moi à…** pruh·nay·mwah ah…
I'm going to…	**Je vais à…** zhuh vay zah…
– this address	**– cette adresse** seh tah·drehs
– the airport	**– l'aéroport** lah·ay·roh·pohr
– the train [railway] station	**– la gare** lah gahr
I'm late.	**Je suis en retard.** zhuh swee zawN ruh·tahr
Can you drive *faster/slower?*	**Pouvez-vous conduire *plus/moins* vite?** poo·vay·voo kohN·dweer plew/mwehN veet
Stop/Wait here.	**Arrêtez/Attendez ici.** ah·ray·tay/ah·tawN·day ee·see
How much?	**Combien ça fait?** kohN·beeyehN sah fay
You said it would cost…	**Vous aviez dit que cela coûterait…** voo zah·veeyay dee kuh suh·lah koo·tuh·ray…
Keep the change.	**Gardez la monnaie.** gahr·day lah moh·nay

You May Hear…

Pour où? poor oo — Where to?

Quelle est l'adresse? keh lay lah·drehs — What's the address?

Il y a une surcharge *le soir/pour l'aéroport*. eel·yah ewn sewr·shahrzh luh swahr/poor lah·ay·roh·pohr — There's a *nighttime/ airport* surcharge.

31

i

A taxi can be hailed on the street; available taxis can be spotted by the lit sign on the roof of the car. You can also wait for a taxi at stands, commonly located near train stations, **métro** stations and other tourist spots.

Though tipping the driver isn't the norm, it's nice to do so for good service. There is usually a surcharge for each piece of luggage. The rate per kilometer may be different at night and for trips to the airport.

Car

Car Rental [Hire]

Where's the car rental [hire]?	**Où est l'agence de location de voitures?** oo ay lah·zhawNs duh loh·kah·seeyohN duh wwah·tewr
I'd like…	**Je voudrais…** zhuh voo·dray…
– a *cheap/small* car	– **une *voiture bon marché/petite voiture*** ewn vwah·tewr bohN mahr·shay/puh·teet vwah·tewr
– an automatic/ a manual	– **une *automatique/manuelle*** ewn oh·toh·mah·teek/mah·new·ehl
– air conditioning	– **la climatisation** lah klee·mah·tee·zah·seeyohN
– a car seat	– **un siège bébé** uhN seeyehzh bay·bay
How much…?	**Combien ça coûte…?** kohN·beeyehN sah koot…
– per *day/week*	– **par *jour/semaine*** pahr zhoor/suh·mehN
– per kilometer	– **par kilomètre** pahr kee·loh·meh·truh
– for unlimited mileage	– **pour un kilométrage illimité** poor uhN kee·loh·meh·trahzh ee·lee·mee·tay
– with insurance	– **avec assurance** ah·vehk ah·sew·rawNs
Are there any discounts?	**Y-a-t-il des réductions?** yah·teel day ray·dewk·seeyohN

32

You May Hear...

Avez-vous un permis de conduire international? ah·vay·voo uhN pehr·mee duh kohN·dweer ehN·tehr·nah·seeyoh·nahl

Do you have an international driver's license?

Votre passeport, s'il vous plaît. voh·truh pahs·pohr seel voo play

Your passport, please.

Voulez-vous prendre une assurance? Voo·lay·voo prawN·druh ewn ah·sew·rawNs

Do you want insurance?

J'ai besoin d'un acompte. zhay buh·zwehN duhN ah·kohNt

I'll need a deposit.

Vos initiales/Signez ici. voh zee·nee·seeyahl/see·nyay zee·see

Initial/Sign here.

Gas [Petrol] Station

Where's the gas [petrol] station?

Où est la station service? oo ay lah stah·seeyohN sehr·vees

Fill it up.

Faites-le plein. feht·luh plehN

...euros, please.

...euros, s'il vous plaît. ...uh·roh seel voo play

I'll pay *in cash/by credit card.*

Je paierai *en espèces/par carte de crédit.* zhuh pay·ray *awN nehs·pehs/pahr kahrt duh kray·dee*

▶ For numbers, see page 173.

You May See...

ESSENCE	gas [petrol]
SANS PLOMB	unleaded
ORDINAIRE	regular
SUPER	super
GAZOLE	diesel

Asking Directions

Is this the way to…?	**Est-ce le chemin pour…?** ehs luh shuh·mehN poor…
How far is it to…?	**À quelle distance se trouve…?** ah kehl dees·tawNs suh troov…
Where's…?	**Où est…?** oo ay…
– …Street	**– la rue…** lah rew…
– this address	**– cette adresse** seh tah·drehs
– the highway [motorway]	**– l'autoroute** loh·toh·root
Can you show me on the map?	**Pouvez-vous me montrer sur la carte?** poo·vay·voo muh mohN·tray sewr lah kahrt
I'm lost.	**Je suis perdu♂/perdue♀.** zhuh swee pehr·dew

You May Hear…

tout droit too drwah	straight ahead
à gauche ah gohsh	left
à droite ah drwaht	right
au coin oh kwehN	around the corner
à l'opposé ah loh·poh·zay	opposite
derrière deh·reeyehr	behind
près de pray duh	next to
après ah·pray	after
nord/sud nohr/sewd	north/south
est/ouest ehst/oowehst	east/west
au feu tricolore oh fuh tree·koh·lohr	at the traffic light
à l'intersection ah lehN·tehr·sehk·seeyohN	at the intersection

You May See...

STOP	**STOP**	stop
	CÉDEZ LE PASSAGE	yield
	STATIONNEMENT INTERDIT	no parking
	SENS UNIQUE	one way
	SENS INTERDIT	no entry
	CIRCULATION INTERDITE	no vehicles allowed
	INTERDICTION DE DÉPASSER	no passing
	FEU TRICOLORE	traffic signal ahead
	SORTIE	exit

Parking

Can I park here?	**Puis-je me garer ici?** pwee·zhuh muh gah·ray ee·see
Where's…?	**Où est…?** oo ay…
– the parking garage	– **le garage** luh gah·rahzh
– the parking lot [car park]	– **le parking** luh pahr·keeng
– the parking meter	– **l'horodateur** loh·roh·dah·tuhr
How much…?	**Combien ça coûte…?** kohN·beeyehN sah koot…
– per hour	– **par heure** pahr uhr
– per day	– **par jour** pahr zhoor
– for overnight	– **toute la nuit** toot lah nwee

> *i*
>
> Parking in larger cities is sometimes hard to find. Parking on the street is possible; you'll usually have to purchase a ticket from a machine for a certain length of time and display it in your windshield. Parking is not allowed on red marked areas or near yellow-marked curbs. Parking garages can be found in downtown areas, though their rates can be expensive.

Breakdown and Repairs

My car *broke down/ won't start*.	**Ma voiture *est tombée en panne/ne démarre pas*.** mah vwah·tewr ay tohN·bay awN pahn/nuh day·mahr pah
Can you fix it (today)?	**Pouvez-vous y réparer (aujourd'hui)?** poo·vay·voo ee ray·pah·ray (oh·zhoor·dwee)
When will it be ready?	**Quand cela sera-t-il prêt?** kawN suh·lah suh·rah·teel pray
How much?	**Combien ça coûte?** kohN·beeyehN sah koot

Accidents

There was an accident.	**Il y a eu un accident.** eel·yah ew uhN nahk· see·dawN
Call *an ambulance/ the police.*	**Appelez *une ambulance/la police.*** ah·puh·lay *ewn nawN·bew·lawNs/lah poh·lees*

Accommodations

Essential

Can you recommend a hotel?	**Pouvez-vous me conseiller un hôtel?** poo·vay·voo muh kohN·say·yay uhN noh·tehl
I made a reservation.	**J'ai fait une réservation.** zhay fay ewn ray·zehr·vah·seeyohN
My name is...	**Mon nom est...** mohN nohN may...
Do you have a room...?	**Avez-vous une chambre...?** ah·vay·voo ewn shawN·bruh...
– for *one/two*	– **pour *un/deux*** poor *uhN/duh*
– with a bathroom	– **avec salle de bains** ah·vehk sahl duh behN
– with air conditioning	– **avec climatisation** ah·vehk klee·mah·tee·zah·seeyohN
For...	**Pour...** poor...
– tonight	– **ce soir** suh swahr
– two nights	– **deux nuits** duh nwee
– one week	– **une semaine** ewn suh·mehn
How much?	**Combien ça coûte?** kohN·beeyehN sah koot
Is there anything cheaper?	**N'y-a-t-il rien de moins cher?** Nee·yah·teel reeyehN duh mwehN shehr
When's check-out?	**Quand dois-je quitter la chambre?** kawN dwah·zhuh kee·tay lah shawN·bruh

Can I leave this in the safe?	**Puis-je laisser ceci dans le coffre?** pwee·zhuh lay·say suh·see dawN luh koh·fruh
Can I leave my bags?	**Puis-je laisser mes bagages?** pwee·zhuh lay·say meh bah·gahzh
Can I have *my bill/a receipt*?	**Puis-je avoir *ma facture/un reçu*?** pwee·zhuh ah·vwahr *mah fahk·tewr/uhN ruh·sew*
I'll pay *in cash/by credit card*.	**Je paierai *en espèces/par carte de crédit*.** zhuh pay·ray *awN nehs·pehs/pahr kahrt duh kray·dee*

If you didn't reserve accommodations before your trip, visit the local **Office de Tourisme** (Tourist Information Office) for recommendations on places to stay.

Finding Lodging

Can you recommend…?	**Pouvez-vous me conseiller…?** poo·vay·voo muh kohN·say·yay…
– a hotel	**– un hôtel** uhN noh·tehl
– a hostel	**– une auberge de jeunesse** ewn oh·behrzh duh zhuh·nehs
– a campsite	**– un camping** uhN kawN·peeng
– a bed and breakfast	**– un bed and breakfast** uhN behd ahnd brayk·fahst
What is it near?	**C'est près de quoi?** say pray duh kwah
How do I get there?	**Comment est-ce que je m'y rends?** koh·mawN ehs kuh zhuh mee rawN

_i_ Hotels in France are ranked in categories or stars; the higher the category or number of stars, the more luxurious and expensive the hotel. **Relais** and **châteaux** are former castles, monasteries, manor houses or abbeys that have been converted into high-end accommodations. **Gîtes-chambres d'hôte** are rentable guestrooms, usually in a village home or on a farm, sometimes referred to as agritourism. Condos, apartments and villas are available for those with larger groups or families or who are staying in one place for at least a week. Hostels and campsites are also available.

At the Hotel

I have a reservation.	**J'ai une réservation.** zhay ewn ray·zehr·vah·seeyohN
My name is…	**Mon nom est…** mohN nohN may…

Do you have a room...?	**Avez-vous une chambre...?** ah·vay·voo ewn shawN·bruh...
– with a *bathroom [toilet]/shower*	– **avec *toilettes/douche*** ah·vehk twah·leht / doosh
– with air conditioning	– **climatisée** klee·mah·tee·zay
– that's smoking/ non-smoking	– **fumeur/non-fumeur** few·muhr/ nohN·few·muhr
For...	**Pour...** poor...
– tonight	– **ce soir** suh swahr
– two nights	– **deux nuits** duh nwee
– a week	– **une semaine** ewn suh·mehn

▶ For numbers, see page 173.

Do you have...?	**Avez-vous...?** ah·vay·voo...
– a computer	– **un ordinateur** uhN nohr·dee·nah·tuhr
– an elevator [a lift]	– **un ascenseur** uhN nah·sawN·suhr
– (wireless) internet service	– **une connexion internet (Wi-Fi)** ewn koh·nek·seeyohN ehN·tehr·neht (wee·fee)
– room service	– **un service de chambres** uhN sehr·vees duh shawN·bruh
– a pool	– **une piscine** ewn pee·seen
– a gym	– **une salle de gym** ewn sahl duh zheem
I need...	**J'ai besoin...** zhay buh·zwehN...
– an extra bed	– **d'un lit supplémentaire** duhN lee sew·play·mawN·tehr
– a cot	– **d'un lit pliant** duhN lee plee·yawN
– a crib	– **d'un berceau** duhN behr·soh

You May Hear…

Votre *passeport/carte de crédit*, s'il vous plaît. voh·truh *pahs·pohr/kahrt duh kray·dee* seel voo play

Your *passport/credit card*, please.

Remplissez ce formulaire. rawN·plee·say suh fohr·mew·lehr

Fill out this form.

Signez ici. see·nyay ee·see

Sign here.

Price

How much per *night/week*?

Combien par *nuit/semaine*? kohN·beeyehN pahr *nwee/suh·mehn*

Does that include *breakfast/sales tax [VAT]*?

Est-ce que cela comprend *le petit déjeuner/la TVA*? ehs kuh suh·lah kohN·prawN luh puh·tee day·zhuh·nay/lah tay·vay·ah

Are there any discounts?

Y-a-t-il des réductions? yah·teel deh ray·dewk·seeyohN

Decisions

Can I see the room?

Puis-je voir la chambre? pwee·zhuh vwahr lah shawN·bruh

I'd like a…room.

Je voudrais une chambre… zhuh voo·dray ewn shawN·bruh…

– better

– **plus confortable** plew kohN·fohr·tah·bluh

– bigger

– **plus grande** plew grawNd

– cheaper

– **moins chère** mwehN shehr

– quieter

– **plus calme** plew kahlm

I'll take it.

Je la prends. zhuh lah prawN

No, I won't take it.

Non, je ne la prends pas. nohN zhuh nuh lah prawN pah

Questions

Where *is/are*...?	**Où *est/sont*...?** oo ay/sohN...
– the bar	– **le bar** luh bahr
– the bathrooms [toilets]	– **les toilettes** lay twah·leht
– the elevator [lift]	– **l'ascenseur** lah·sawN·suhr
I'd like...	**Je voudrais...** zhuh voo·dray...
– a blanket	– **une couverture** ewn koo·vehr·tewr
– an iron	– **un fer à repasser** uhN feh rah ruh·pah·say
– the *room key/key card*	– **la *clé/carte* de la chambre** lah klay/kahrt duh lah shawN·bruh
– a pillow	– **un oreiller** uhN noh·reh·yay
– soap	– **du savon** dew sah·vohN
– toilet paper	– **du papier toilette** dew pah·pee·yay twah·leht
– a towel	– **une serviette** ewn sehr·veeyeht
Do you have an adapter for this?	**Avez-vous un adaptateur pour ceci?** ah·vay·voo uhN nah·dahp·tah·tuhr poor suh·see
How do you turn on the lights?	**Comment allume-t-on les lumières?** koh·mawN ah·lewm·tohN lay lew·mee·yehr
Can you wake me at...?	**Pouvez-vous me réveiller à...?** poo·vay·voo muh ray·veh·yay ah...
Can I leave this in the safe?	**Puis-je laisser ceci dans le coffre?** pwee·zhuh lay·say suh·see dawN luh koh·fruh
Can I have my things from the safe?	**Puis-je prendre mes affaires qui sont dans le coffre?** pwee·zhuh prawN·druh meh zah·fehr kee sohN dawN luh koh·fruh
Is there *mail [post]/a message* for me?	**Y-a-t-il *du courrier/un message* pour moi?** yah·teel dew koo·reeyay/uhN meh·sahzh poor mwah

You May See…

POUSSER/TIRER	push/pull
TOILETTES	bathroom [toilet]
DOUCHES	showers
ASCENSEUR	elevator [lift]
ESCALIERS	stairs
DISTRIBUTEURS	vending machines
GLACE	ice
TEINTURERIE	laundry
NE PAS DÉRANGER	do not disturb
PORTE COUPE-FEU	fire door
SORTIE (DE SECOURS)	(emergency) exit
APPEL RÉVEIL	wake-up call

Problems

There's a problem.	**Il y a un problème.** eel·yah uhN proh·blehm
I lost my *key/key card.*	**J'ai perdu la *clé/carte* de ma chambre.** zhay pehr·dew lah *klay/kahrt* duh mah shawN·bruh
I've locked my *key/key card* in the room.	**J'ai laissé ma *clé/carte* à l'intérieur de ma chambre.** zhay leh·say mah *klay/kahrt* ah lehN·tay·reeyuhr duh mah shawN·bruh
There's no *hot water/toilet paper.*	**Il n'y a pas *d'eau chaude/de papier toilette.*** eel nee·yah pah *doh shohd/duh pah·pee·yay twah·leht*
The room is dirty.	**La chambre est sale.** lah shawN·bruh ay sahl
There are bugs in the room.	**Il y a des insectes dans la chambre.** eel·yah day zehN·sehkt dawN lah shawN·bruh
…doesn't work.	**…ne fonctionne pas.** …nuh fohNk·seeyohn pah

43

Can you fix...?	**Pouvez-vous réparer...?** poo·vay·voo ray·pah·ray...
– the air conditioning	– **la climatisation** lah klee·mah·tee·zah·seeyohN
– the fan	– **le ventilateur** luh vawN·tee·lah·tuhr
– the heat [heating]	– **le chauffage** luh shoh·fahzh
– the light	– **la lumière** lah lew·mee·yehr
– the TV	– **la télé** lah tay·lay
– the toilet	– **les toilettes** lay twah·leht
I'd like another room.	**Je voudrais une autre chambre.** zhuh voo·dray zewn oh·truh shawN·bruh

---

i Unlike the U.S., most of Europe runs on 220-volt electricity, and plugs are two-pronged. You may need a converter and/or an adapter for your appliance.

Check-out

When's check-out?	**Quand dois-je quitter la chambre?** kawN dwah·zhuh kee·tay lah shawN·bruh
Can I leave my bags here until...?	**Puis-je laisser mes bagages ici jusqu'à...?** pwee·zhuh leh·say meh bah·gahzh ee·see zhew·skah...
Can I have *an itemized bill/ a receipt*?	**Puis-je avoir *une facture détaillée/un reçu*?** pwee·zhuh ah·vwahr *ewn fahk·tewr day·tie·yay/uhN ruh·sew*
I think there's a mistake.	**Je pense qu'il y a une erreur.** zhuh pawNs keel·yah ewn ay·ruhr
I'll pay *in cash/by credit card*.	**Je paierai *en espèces/par carte de crédit*.** zhuh pay·ray *awN nehs·pehs/pahr kahrt duh kray·dee*

i It is customary to give a tip to porters, hotel bartenders, room service staff and maids; however, this is not a set rule so ask at the reception desk. You should tip the porter €1-1.50 per piece of luggage. A tip of €1.50 per day is adequate for maid service. Room service employees and bartenders can be tipped an extra €0.50-1 if service was good; the customary tip amount is already included in the total of your bill.

Renting

I reserved *an apartment/a room.*	**J'ai réservé *un appartement/une chambre.*** zhay ray·zehr·vay uhN nah·pahrt·mawN/ewn shawN·bruh
My name is…	**Je m'appelle…** zhuh mah·pehl…
Can I have the keys?	**Puis-je avoir les clés?** pwee·zhuh ah·vwahr lay klay
Are there…?	**Y-a-t-il des…?** yah·teel day…
– dishes	**– assiettes** ah·seeyeht
– pillows	**– oreillers** oh·reh·yay
– sheets	**– draps** drah
– towels	**– serviettes** sehr·veeyeht
– kitchen utensils	**– ustensiles de cuisine** ews·tawN·seel duh kwee·zeen
When do I put out the *trash [rubbish]/recycling?*	**Quand dois-je sortir les *poubelles/ordures à recycler?*** kawN dwah·zhuh sohr·teer lay poo·behl/zohr·dewr ah ruh·seek·lay
…is broken.	**…est cassé♂/cassée♀.** …ay kah·say

How does... work?	**Comment fonctionne...?** koh·mawN fohNk·seeyohn...
– the air conditioner	– **la climatisation** lah klee·mah·tee·zah·seeyohN
– the dishwasher	– **le lave-vaisselle** luh lahv·veh·sehl
– the freezer	– **le congélateur** luh kohN·zhay·lah·tuhr
– the heater	– **le chauffage** luh shoh·fahzh
– the microwave	– **le micro-onde** luh mee·kroh·ohNd
– the refrigerator	– **le réfrigérateur** luh ray·free·zhay·rah·tuhr
– the stove	– **la gazinière** lah gah·zee·neeyehr
– the washing machine	– **la machine à laver** lah mah·sheen ah lah·vay

Household Items

I need...	**J'ai besoin...** zhay buh·zwehN...
– an adapter	– **d'un adaptateur** duhN nah·dahp·tah·tuhr
– aluminum [kitchen] foil	– **de papier aluminium** duh pah·peeyay ah·lew·mee·neeyewm
– a bottle opener	– **d'un ouvre-bouteille** duhN oo·vruh·boo·tehy
– a broom	– **d'un balai** duhN bah·lay
– a can opener	– **d'un ouvre boîte** duhN noo·vruh bwaht
– cleaning supplies	– **de produits d'entretien** duh proh·dwee dawN·truh·teeyehN
– a corkscrew	– **d'un tire-bouchon** duhN teer·boo·shohN
– detergent	– **de détergent** duh day·tehr·zhawN
– dishwashing liquid	– **de détergent pour lave-vaisselle** duh day·tehr·zhawN poor lahv·veh·sehl
– garbage [rubbish] bags	– **de sacs poubelles** duh sahk poo·behl
– a lightbulb	– **d'une ampoule** dewn nawN·pool

– matches	– **d'allumettes** dah·lew·meht
– a mop	– **d'une serpillière** dewn sehr·peeyehr
– napkins	– **de serviettes de tables** duh sehr·veeyeht duh tah·bluh
– paper towels	– **de serviettes en papier** duh sehr·veeyeht awN pah·peeyay
– plastic wrap [cling film]	– **de cellophane** duh seh·loh·fahn
– a plunger	– **d'un déboucheur de toilettes** duhN day·boo·shur duh twah·leht
– scissors	– **de ciseaux** duh see·zoh
– a vacuum cleaner	– **d'un aspirateur** duhN nah·spee·rah·tuhr

▶ For dishes and utensils, see page 68.

▶ For oven temperatures, see page 181.

Hostel

Is there a bed available?	**Y-a-t-il un lit de libre?** yah·teel uhN lee duh lee·bruh
I'd like…	**Je voudrais…** zhuh voo·dray…
– a *single/double* room	– **une chambre *simple/double*** ewn shawN·bruh *sehN·pluh/doo·bluh*
– a blanket	– **une couverture** ewn koo·vehr·tewr
– a pillow	– **un oreiller** uhN noh·reh·yay
– sheets	– **des draps** day drah
– a towel	– **une serviette de bain** ewn sehr·veeyeht duh behN
Do you have lockers?	**Avez-vous des cadenas?** ah·vay·voo day cah·duh·nah
When do you lock up?	**Quand fermez-vous?** kawN fehr·may·voo

Do I need a membership card?	**Ai-je besoin d'une carte de membre?** ay·zhuh buh·zwehN dewn kahrt duh mawN·bruh
Here's my international student card.	**Voici ma carte internationale d'étudiant.** vwah·see mah kahrt ehN·tehr·nah·seeyoh·nahl day·tew·deeyawN

> *i* Present your accredited Youth Hostel Association card to stay in a French hostel run by the **Fédération Unie des Auberges de Jeunesse (FUAJ)** or the **Ligue Française pour les Auberges de Jeunesse (LFAJ)**. **Gîtes d'Étapes** offer hostel accommodations, usually in or near national parks, that are popular with hikers; no membership is needed to stay in these.
>
> Hostels fill up quickly during tourist seasons; make reservations well in advance. Many hostels accept online reservations.

Camping

Can I camp here?	**Puis-je camper ici?** pwee·zhuh kawN·pay ee·see
Where's the campsite?	**Où est le camping?** oo ay luh kawN·peeng
What is the charge per *day/week*?	**Quel est le prix par *jour/semaine*?** keh lay luh pree pahr *zhoor/suh·mehn*
Are there...?	**Y-a-t-il...?** yah·teel...
– cooking facilities	– **des cuisines** day kwee·zeen
– electric outlets	– **des prises électriques** day pree zay·lehk·treek
– laundry facilities	– **des buanderies** day bew·awN·dree
– showers	– **des douches** day doosh
– tents for rent [hire]	– **des tentes à louer** day tawN tah looway
Where can I empty the chemical toilet?	**Où puis-je vider les toilettes portables?** oo pwee·zhuh vee·day lay twah·leht pohr·tah·bluh

You May See...

EAU POTABLE	drinking water
CAMPING INTERDIT	no camping
FEUX DE BOIS/BARBECUES INTERDITS	no *fires/barbecues*

▶ For household items, see page 46.

▶ For dishes, utensils and kitchen tools, see page 68.

Internet and Communications

Essential

Where's an internet cafe?	**Où y-a-t-il un cyber café?** oo yah·teel uhN see·behr kah·fay
Can I *access the internet/check my e-mail*?	**Puis-je *me connecter à Internet/consulter mes mails*?** pwee·zhuh muh koh·nehk·tay ah ehN·tehr·neht/kohN·sewl·tay may mehyl
How much per *half hour/hour*?	**Combien coûte *la demi-heure/l'heure*?** kohN·beeyehN koot lah duh·mee·uhr/luhr
How do I *connect/log on*?	**Comment est-ce que *je me connecte/j'ouvre une session*?** koh·mawN ehs kuh zhuh muh koh·nehkt/zhoo·vruh ewn seh·seeyohN
A phone card, please.	**Une carte de téléphone, s'il vous plaît.** ewn kahrt duh tay·lay·fohn seel voo play
Can I have your phone number?	**Puis-je avoir votre numéro de téléphone?** pwee·zhuh ah·vwahr voh·truh new·meh·roh duh tay·lay·fohn
Here's my *number/e-mail*.	**Voici mon *numéro/mail*.** vwah·see mohN new·meh·roh/mehyl
Call me.	**Appelle-moi.** ah·pehl·mwah

E-mail me.	**Envoie-moi un mail.** awN·vwah·mwah uhN mehyl
Hello. This is…	**Bonjour. C'est…** bohN·zhoor say…
Can I speak to…?	**Puis-je parler à…?** pwee·zhuh pahr·lay ah…
Can you repeat that?	**Pouvez-vous répéter cela?** poo·vay·voo ray·pay·tay suh·lah
I'll call back later.	**Je rappellerai plus tard.** zhuh rah·peh·luh·ray plew tahr
Bye.	**Au revoir.** oh ruh·vwahr
Where's the post office?	**Où est la poste?** oo ay lah pohst
I'd like to send this to…	**Je voudrais envoyer ceci à…** zhuh voo·dray zawN·vwah·yay suh·see ah…

> **i** French language purists prefer to avoid using words adopted directly from English, but their best efforts can't always change popular usage. Even though you may see and hear the official dictionary-approved word for e-mail, **courriel** (short for **courriel-électronique**, electronic mail), the word **mail** is the one most often used in France and what you will see used throughout this book.

Computer, Internet and E-Mail

Where's an internet cafe?	**Où y-a-t-il un cyber café?** oo yah·teel uhN see·behr kah·fay
Does it have wireless internet?	**Est-ce qu'il a la connexion Wi-Fi?** ehs kee·lee ah lah koh·nehk·seeyohN wee·fee

Can you show me how to turn *on/off* the computer?	**Pouvez-vous me montrer comment *allumer/éteindre* l'ordinateur?** poo·vay·voo muh mohN·tray koh·mawN *ah·lew·may/ eh·tehyuhn·druh* lohr·dee·nah·tuhr
Can I…?	**Puis-je…?** pwee·zhuh…
– access the internet	**– accéder à Internet** ahk·seh·day ah ehN·tehr·neht
– check my e-mail	**– consulter mes mails** kohN·sewl·tay may mehyl
– print	**– imprimer** ehN·pree·may
How much per *half hour/hour*?	**Combien coûte *la demi-heure/ l'heure*?** kohN·beeyehN koot *lah duh·mee·uhr/luhr*

How do I...?	**Comment est-ce que...?** koh·mawN ehs kuh...
– connect/disconnect	– **je me *connecte/déconnecte*** zhuh muh koh·nehkt/day·koh·nehkt
– log *on/off*	– ***j'ouvre/je termine* la session** zhoo·vruh/zhuh tehr·meen lah seh·seeyohN
– type this symbol	– **je frappe ce symbole** zhuh frahp suh sehN·bohl
What's your e-mail?	**Quel est votre mail?** keh lay voh·truh mehyl
My e-mail is...	**Mon mail est...** mohN mehyl ay...
Do you have a scanner?	**Avez-vous un scanneur?** ah·vay·voo uhN skah·nuhr

You May See...

FERMER	close
SUPPRIMER	delete
MAIL	e-mail
SORTIR	exit
AIDE	help
MESSAGERIE INSTANTANÉE	instant messenger
INTERNET	internet
OUVRIR UNE SESSION	log in
NOUVEAU (MESSAGE)	new (message)
ALLUMÉ/ÉTEINT	on/off
OUVRIR	open
IMPRIMER	print
SAUVEGARDER	save
ENVOYER	send
NOM UTILISATEUR/MOT DE PASSE	username/password
CONNEXION WI-FI	wireless internet

Phone

A *phone card/ prepaid phone*, please.	**Une *carte de téléphone/téléphone prépayée*, s'il vous plaît.** ewn *kahrt duh tay·lay·fohn/tay·lay·fohn pray·pay·yay* seel voo play
How much?	**Combien ça coûte?** kohN·beeyehN sah koot
Where's the pay phone?	**Où y-a-t-il une cabine téléphonique?** oo yah·teel ewn kah·been tay·lay·foh·neek
My phone doesn't work here.	**Mon téléphone est en panne.** mohN tay·lay·fohn ay awN pahn
What's the *area/ country* code for…?	**Quel est le code *régional/national* pour…?** keh lay luh kohd *ray·zheeyoh·nahl/ nah·seeyoh·nahl* poor…

What's the number for Information?	**Quel est le numéro des renseignements?** keh lay luh new·may·roh day rawN·seh·nyuh·mawN
I'd like the number for...	**Puis-je avoir le numéro de...** pwee·zhuh ah·vwahr luh new·may·roh duh...
I'd like to call collect [reverse the charges].	**Je voudrais appeler en PCV.** zhuh voo·dray zah·puh·lay awN pay·say·vay
Can I have your number?	**Puis-je avoir votre numéro?** pwee·zhuh ah·vwahr voh·truh new·meh·roh
Here's my number.	**Voici mon numéro.** vwah·see mohN new·may·roh

▶ For numbers, see page 173.

Please *call/text* me.	**S'il vous plaît, *appelez-moi/envoyez-moi un SMS.*** seel voo play ah·puh·lay·mwah/ awN·vwah·yay·mwah uhN ehs·ehm·ehs
I'll *call/text* you.	**Je vous *appellerai/enverrai un SMS.*** zhuh voo zah·peh·luh·ray/zawN·veh·ray uhN nehs·ehm·ehs

On the Phone

Hello. This is...	**Bonjour. C'est...** bohN·zhoor say...
Can I speak to...?	**Puis-je parler à...?** pwee·zhuh pahr·lay ah...
Extension...	**Poste...** pohst...
Speak *louder/more slowly*, please.	**Parlez plus *fort/lentement,* s'il vous plaît.** pahr·lay plew *fohr/lawN·tuh·mawN* seel voo play
Can you repeat that?	**Pouvez-vous répéter cela?** poo·vay·voo ray·pay·tay suh·lah
I'll call back later.	**Je rappellerai plus tard.** zhuh rah·peh·luh·ray plew tahr
Bye.	**Au revoir.** oh ruh·vwahr

You May Hear...

Qui est à l'appareil?
kee ay ah lah·pah·rehy

Who's calling?

Attendez un instant.
ah·tawN·day uhN nehN·stawN

Hold on.

Je vous le ♂/la ♀ passe.
zhuh voo luh ♂/lah ♀ pahs

I'll put you through to him/her.

Il ♂/Elle ♀ n'est pas là/est sur une autre ligne. eel ♂/ehl ♀ nay pah lah/ay sewr ewn oh·truh lee·nyuh

He/She is *not here/on another line*.

Voulez-vous laisser un message?
voo·lay·voo leh·say uhN meh·sahzh

Would you like to leave a message?

Rappelez *plus tard/dans dix minutes*.
rah·puh·lay *plew tahr/dawN dee mee·newt*

Call back *later/in ten minutes*.

Peut-il ♂/Peut-elle ♀ vous rappeler?
puh·teel ♂/puh·tehl ♀ voo rah·puh·lay

Can he/she call you back?

Quel est votre numéro de téléphone?
keh lay voh·truh new·may·roh duh tay·lay·fohn

What's your number?

---

i Most pay phones in France are card operated; some require phone cards, others, credit cards. You can purchase phone cards at **tabacs** (tobacconists), at **la Poste** (the post office) and wherever you see the sign **Télécarte**.

French phone numbers have 10 digits, including a two digit regional prefix. When calling within the country, you must dial all 10 digits, even when dialing within the same region. When dialing from outside the country, delete the first 0 (part of the regional prefix).

To call the U.S. or Canada from France, dial 00 + 1 + area code + phone number. To call the U.K. from France, dial 00 + 44 + area code (minus the first 0) + phone number.

Fax

Can I *send/receive* a fax here?	**Puis-je *envoyer/recevoir* un fax ici?** pwee·zhuh *awN·vwah·yay/ruh·suh·vwah* ruhN fahks ee·see
What's the fax number?	**Quel est le numéro de fax?** keh lay luh new·may·roh duh fahks
Please fax this to…	**S'il vous plaît, faxer ceci au…** seel voo play fahk·say suh·see oh…

Post Office

Where's the *post office/mailbox [postbox]*?	**Où est la *poste/boîte aux lettres*?** oo ay lah *pohst/bwah·toh·leh·truh*
A stamp for this *postcard/letter* to…	**Un timbre pour cette *carte postale/lettre* pour…** uhN tehN·bruh poor seht *kahrt pohs·tahl/leh·truh* poor…
How much?	**Combien ça coûte?** kohN·beeyehN sah koot
Send this package by *airmail/express*.	**Envoyez ce paquet *par avion/en express*.** awN·vwah·yay suh pah·keh *pah rah·veeyohN/ awN ehk·sprehs*
A receipt, please.	**Un reçu, s'il vous plaît.** uhN ruh·sew seel voo play

You May Hear…

Remplissez ce formulaire de déclaration de douane.
rawN·plee·say suh fohr·mew·lehr duh
day·klah·rah·seeyohN duh doo·wahn

Fill out the customs declaration form.

Quelle est la valeur?
keh lay lah vah·luhr

What's the value?

Qu'est-ce qu'il y a à l'intérieur?
kehs keel·yah ah lehN·tay·reeyuhr

What's inside?

Most locations of **la Poste** (the post office) are open from 8 a.m. to 7 or 8 p.m., Monday through Friday. On Saturdays, most post offices close at noon. In addition to standard postal services, you will also be able to bank at **la Poste**; ATMs can be found at many locations.

▼ *Food*

Essential

Can you recommend a good *restaurant/ bar*?	**Pouvez-vous me conseiller un bon *restaurant/bar*?** poo·vay·voo muh kohN·say·yay uhN bohN *reh·stoh·rawN/bahr*
Is there a *traditional French/inexpensive* restaurant nearby?	**Y-a-t-il un restaurant *traditionnel français/ bon marché* près d'ici?** yah·teel uhN reh·stoh·rawN *trah·dee·seeyohN·nehl frawN·say/ bohN mahr·shay* pray dee·see
A table for…, please.	**Une table pour…, s'il vous plaît.** ewn tah·bluh poor…seel voo play
Can we sit…?	**Pouvons-nous nous asseoir…?** poo·vohN·noo noo zah·swahr…
– here/there	– **ici/là** ee·see/lah
– outside	– **dehors** duh·ohr
– in a non-smoking area	– **en zone non-fumeur** awN zohn nohN-few·muhr
I'm waiting for someone.	**J'attends quelqu'un.** zhah·tawN kehl·kuhN
Where are the restrooms [toilets]?	**Où sont les toilettes?** oo sohN lay twah·leht
The menu, please.	**La carte, s'il vous plaît.** lah kahrt seel voo play
What do you recommend?	**Que recommandez-vous?** kuh reh·koh·mawN·day·voo
I'd like…	**Je voudrais…** zhuh voo·dray…
Some more…, please.	**Un peu plus de…, s'il vous plaît.** uhN puh plew duh…seel voo play
Enjoy your meal!	**Bon appétit!** bohN nah·peh·tee

The check [bill], please.	**L'addition, s'il vous plaît.** lah·dee·seeyohN seel voo play
Is service included?	**Est-ce que le service est compris?** ehs kuh luh sehr·vees ay kohN·pree
Can I *pay by credit card/have a receipt*?	**Puis-je *payer par carte de crédit/avoir un reçu*?** pwee·zhuh *pay·yay pahr kahrt duh kray·dee/ah·vwahr uhN ruh·sew*

Restaurant Types

Can you recommend…?	**Pouvez-vous me conseiller…?** poo·vay·voo muh kohN·say·yay…
– a restaurant	**– un restaurant** uhN reh·stoh·rawN
– a bar	**– un bar** uhN bahr
– a café	**– un café** uhN kah·fay
– a fast-food place	**– un fast-food** uhN fahst·food

Reservations and Questions

I'd like to reserve a table…	**Je voudrais réserver une table…** zhuh voo·dray ray·zehr·vay ewn tah·bluh…
– for two	**– pour deux** poor duh
– for this evening	**– pour ce soir** poor suh swahr
– for tomorrow at…	**– pour demain à…** poor duh·mehN ah…
A table for two, please.	**Une table pour deux, s'il vous plaît.** ewn tah·bluh poor duh seel voo play
I have a reservation.	**J'ai une réservation.** zhay ewn ray·zehr·vah·seeyohN
My name is…	**Mon nom est…** mohN nohN may…
Can we sit…?	**Pouvons-nous nous asseoir…?** poo·vohN·noo noo zah·swahr…
– here/there	**– ici/là** ee·see/lah

– outside	**– dehors** duh·ohr
– in a non-smoking area	**– en zone non-fumeur** awN zohn nohN·few·muhr
– by the window	**– à côté de la fenêtre** ah koh·tay duh lah fuh·neh·truh
Where are the restrooms [toilets]?	**Où sont les toilettes?** oo sohN lay twah·leht

You May Hear...

Avez-vous réservé? ah·vay·voo ray·zehr·vay

Do you have a reservation?

Pour combien? poor kohN·beeyehN

How many?

Fumeur ou non-fumeur? few·muhr oo nohN·few·muhr

Smoking or non-smoking?

Êtes-vous prêts (à commander)? eht·voo preh (ah koh·mawN·day)

Are you ready (to order)?

Que désirez-vous? kuh day·zee·ray·voo

What would you like?

Je vous conseille... zhuh voo kohN·sehy...

I recommend...

Bon appétit. bohN nah·peh·tee

Enjoy your meal.

Ordering

Excuse me, *sir/ma'am*?

S'il vous plaît, *monsieur/madame*? seel voo play *muh·seeyuhr/mah·dahm*

We're ready (to order).

Nous sommes prêts (à commander). noo sohm preh (ah koh·mawN·day)

The wine list, please.

La liste des vins, s'il vous plaît. lah leest day vehN seel voo play

I'd like...

Je voudrais... zhuh voo·dray...

– a bottle of...

– une bouteille de... ewn boo·tehy duh...

– a carafe of...

– une carafe de... ewn kah·rahf duh...

– a glass of...

– un verre de... uhN vehr duh...

▶ For alcoholic and non-alcoholic drinks, see page 85.

The menu, please.

La carte, s'il vous plaît. lah kahrt seel voo play

Do you have...?

Avez-vous...? ah·vay voo...

– a menu in English

– un menu en anglais uhN muh·new awN nawN·glay

– a fixed-price menu	– **un menu à prix fixe** uhN muh·new ah pree feeks
– a children's menu	– **un menu enfant** uhN muh·new awN·fawN
What do you recommend?	**Que me conseillez-vous?** kuh muh kohN·say·yay·voo
What's this?	**Qu'est-ce que c'est?** kehs kuh say
What's in it?	**Quels sont les ingrédients?** kehl sohN lay zehN·gray·deeyehN
Is it spicy?	**C'est épicé?** say ay·pee·say
Without…, please.	**Sans…, s'il vous plaît.** sawN…seel voo play
It's to go [take away].	**C'est pour emporter.** say poor awN·pohr·tay

You May See...

COUVERT	cover charge
PRIX FIXE	fixed-price
MENU (DU JOUR)	menu (of the day)
SERVICE (NON) COMPRIS	service (not) included
MENU À LA CARTE	specials

Cooking Methods

baked	**cuit** kwee
boiled	**bouilli** boo·yee
braised	**braisé** bray·zay
breaded	**en croute** awN kroot
creamed	**à la crème** ah lah krehm
diced	**en rondelles** awN rohN·dehl

filleted	**en filets** awN fee·lay
fried	**frit** free
grilled	**grillé** gree·yay
poached	**poché** poh·shay
roasted	**rôti** roh·tee
sautéed	**poêlé** pwah·lay
smoked	**fumé** few·may
steamed	**à la vapeur** ah lah vah·puhr
stewed	**mijoté** mee·zhoh·tay
stuffed	**farci** fahr·see

Special Requirements

I'm...	**Je suis...** zhuh swee...
– diabetic	– **diabétique** deeyah·beh·teek
– lactose intolerant	– **allergique au lactose** ah·lehr·zheek oh lahk·tohz
– vegetarian	– **végétarien** ♂/**végétarienne** ♀ vay·zhay·tah·reeyehN ♂/vay·zhay·tah·reeyehn ♀
– vegan	– **végétalien** vay·zhay·tah·leeyehN
I'm allergic to...	**Je suis allergique à...** zhuh swee ah·lehr·zheek ah...
I can't eat...	**Je ne peux pas manger...** zhuh nuh puh pah mawN·zhay...
– dairy products	– **de produits laitiers** duh proh·dwee lay·teeyay
– gluten	– **de gluten** duh glew·tawN
– nuts	– **des noix** day nwah
– pork	– **du porc** dew pohr
– shellfish	– **des fruits de mer** day frwee duh mehr

– spicy foods	– **de la nourriture épicée** duh lah noo·ree·tewr ay·pee·say
– wheat	– **du blé** dew blay
Is it *halal/kosher*?	**Est-ce que c'est *halal/casher*?** ehs kuh say ah·lahl/kah·shehr

Dining with Kids

Do you have children's portions?	**Faites-vous des portions enfants?** feht·voo day pohr·seeyohN awN·fawN
A *highchair/child's seat*, please.	*Une chaise haute pour bébé/Un siège pour enfant*, s'il vous plaît. *ewn shay zoht poor bay·bay/uhN seeyehzh poo rawN·fawN* seel voo play
Where can I *feed/change* the baby?	**Où puis-je *allaiter/changer* le bébé?** oo pwee·zhuh ah·leh·tay/shawN·zhay luh bay·bay
Can you warm this?	**Pouvez-vous réchauffer ceci?** poo·vay·voo ray·shoh·fay suh·see

▶For travel with children, see page 148.

Complaints

When will our food be ready?	**Dans combien de temps serons-nous servis?** dawN kohN·beeyehN duh tawN suh·rohN·noo sehr·vee
We can't wait any longer.	**Nous ne pouvons plus attendre.** noo nuh poo·vohN plew zhah·tawN·druh
We're leaving.	**Nous partons.** noo pahr·tohN
I didn't order this.	**Ce n'est pas ce que j'ai commandé.** suh nay pah suh kuh zhay koh·mawN·day
I ordered...	**J'ai commandé...** zhay koh·mawN·day...
I can't eat this.	**Je ne peux pas manger ça.** zhuh nuh puh pah mawN·zhay sah

This is too...	C'est trop... say troh...
– cold/hot	– **froid/chaud** frwah/shoh
– salty/spicy	– **salé/épicé** sah·lay/ay·pee·say
– tough/bland	– **dur/sans goût** dewr/sawN goo
This isn't *clean/fresh*.	**Ce n'est pas *propre/frais*.** suh nay pah *proh·pruh/fray*

Paying

The check [bill], please.	**L'addition, s'il vous plaît.** lah·dee·seeyohN seel voo play
Separate checks [bills], please.	**Des additions séparées, s'il vous plaît.** day zah·dee·seeyohN say·pah·ray seel voo play
It's all together.	**C'est ensemble.** say tawN·sawN·bluh
Is service included?	**Le service est-il compris?** luh sehr·vees ay·teel kohN·pree
What's this amount for?	**À quoi correspond ce montant?** ah kwah koh·rhes·pohN suh mohN·tawN
I didn't have that. I had...	**Je n'ai pas eu ceci. J'ai eu...** zhuh nay pah ew suh·see zhay ew...
Can I have *a receipt/ an itemized bill*?	**Puis-je avoir un *reçu/reçu détaillé*?** pwee·zhuh ah·vwahr uhN *ruh·sew/ruh·sew day·tie·yay*
That was delicious!	**C'était délicieux!** seh·tay day·lee·seeyuh

Service is included in the price at cafes and restaurants. However, people do tend to leave a small tip. Round up the bill to the nearest euro or two for good service.

Market

Where are the *carts* [trolleys]/*baskets*?	**Où sont les *chariots/paniers*?** oo sohN lay *shah·reeyoh/pah·neeyay*
Where is…?	**Où est…?** oo ay…

▶ For food items, see page 90.

I'd like some of *that/this*.	**Je voudrais un peu de *cela/ceci*.** zhuh voo·dray zuhN puh duh *suh·lah/suh·see*
Can I taste it?	**Puis-je goûter?** pwee·zhuh goo·tay
I'd like…	**Je voudrais…** zhuh voo·dray…
– a *kilo/half-kilo* of…	– **un *kilo/demi-kilo* de…** uhN *kee·loh/duh·mee·kee·loh* duh…
– a liter of…	– **un litre de…** uhN lee·truh duh…
– a piece of…	– **une pièce de…** ewn peeyehs duh…
– a slice of…	– **un morceau de…** uhN mohr·soh duh…
More./Less.	**Plus./Moins.** plew/mwehN
How much?	**Combien ça coûte?** kohN·beeyehN sah koot
Where do I pay?	**Où dois-je payer?** oo dwah·zhuh pay·yay
A bag, please.	**Un sachet, s'il vous plaît.** uhN sah·shay seel voo play
I'm being helped.	**On me sert.** ohN muh sehr

▶ For conversion tables, see page 179.

You May Hear…

Puis-je vous aider? pwee·zhuh voo zay·day	Can I help you?
Que voulez-vous? kuh voo·lay·voo	What would you like?
Autre chose? oh·truh shohz	Anything else?
Ça fait…euros. Sah fay…uh·roh	That's…euros.

i

Local markets—indoor and outdoor—are a wonderful way to discover fresh, seasonal and regional products and to get a hint of the French way of life. Both sell a variety of products such as cheese, meat, flowers, homemade preserves, honey, nuts and farm fresh vegetables, fruit, eggs and more.

You May See...

À CONSOMMER DE PRÉFÉRENCE AVANT LE...	best if used by...
KILOCALORIES	calories
0% DE MATIÈRES GRASSES	fat free
CONSERVER AU RÉFRIGÉRATEUR	keep refrigerated
PEUT CONTENIR DES TRACES DE...	may contain traces of...
VA AU MICRO-ONDE	microwaveable
DATE LIMITE DE VENTE...	sell by...
CONVIENT AUX VÉGÉTARIENS	suitable for vegetarians

Dishes, Utensils and Kitchen Tools

bottle opener	**un décapsuleur**	uhN day·kahp·sew·luhr
bowl	**un saladier**	uhN sah·lah·deeyay
can opener	**un ouvre-boîte**	uhN oo·vruh·bwaht
corkscrew	**un tire-bouchon**	uhN teer·boo·shohN
cup	**une tasse**	ewn tahs

fork	**une fourchette** ewn foor·sheht
frying pan	**une poêle** ewn pwahl
glass	**un verre** uhN vehr
(steak) knife	**un couteau (à steak)** uhN koo·toh (ah stayk)
measuring cup/spoon	**une *mesure/cuillère à doser*** ewn *meh·zewr/ kwee·yehr ah doh·say*
napkin	**une serviette** ewn sayr·veeyeht
plate	**une assiette** ewn ah·seeyeht
pot	**une casserole** ewn kah·suh·rohl
spatula	**une spatule** ewn spah·tewl
spoon	**une cuillère** ewn kwee·yehr

Meals

Le petit déjeuner (breakfast) is usually served from 7 a.m. until 10 a.m. and is a light meal, such as bread with butter and jam and coffee or tea. **Le déjeuner** (lunch) is usually served from noon until 2 p.m. and can be a full sit-down meal or a fast meal on the go, whichever you have time for. A picnic lunch is popular, and all the fixings can be found at the local bakery, butcher and wine store. **Le goûter** (snack), perhaps a croissant or pieces of chocolate, is common in the afternoon, especially for children. **Le dîner** (dinner) is usually served between 7 p.m. and 10 p.m. This often is a multi-course meal, served with wine, and enjoyed at a leisurely pace.

Breakfast

le bacon luh beh·kohn	bacon
le beurre luh buhr	butter
le *café/thé...* luh *kah·fay/tay*...	coffee/tea...
– **noir** nwahr	– black
– **déca** day·kah	– decaf
– **au lait** oh lay	– with milk
– **avec du sucre** ah·vehk dew sew·kruh	– with sugar
– **avec de l'édulcorant** ah·vehk duh lay·dewl·koh·rawN	– with artificial sweetener
les céréales *chaudes/froides* lay say·ray·ahl *shohd/frwahd*	*cold/hot* cereal
la charcuterie lah shahr·kew·tuh·ree	cold cuts [charcuterie]
le croissant luh krwah·sawN	croissant
la confiture lah kohN·fee·tewr	jam/jelly
le fromage luh froh·mahzh	cheese
le jus... luh zhew...	...juice
– **d'orange** doh·rawNzh	– orange
– **de pommes** duh pohm	– apple
– **de pamplemousse** duh pawN·pluh·moos	– grapefruit
le lait luh lay	milk
l'avoine lah·vwahn	oatmeal
l'eau loh	water
le muesli luh mews·lee	granola [muesli]
le muffin luh muh·feen	muffin

I'd like...	**Je voudrais...** zhuh voo·dray...
More..., please.	**Plus..., s'il vous plaît.** plews...seel voo play

l'œuf... luhf...	...egg
– **dur/à la coque** dewr/ah lah kohk	– hard-/soft-boiled
– **sur le plat** sewr luh plah	– fried
– **brouillé** broo·yay	– scrambled
l'**omelette** lohm·leht	omelet
le **pain** luh pehN	bread
le **pain grillé** luh pehN gree·yay	toast
le **petit pain** luh puh·tee pehN	roll
la **saucisse** lah soh·sees	sausage
le **yaourt** luh yah·oort	yogurt

Appetizers [Starters]

les **acras** lay zhah·krah	small, fried fritters made from cod
l'**andouille** lawN·doohy	seasoned sausage, served grilled or fried
la **bouchée à la reine** lah boo·shay ah lah rehn	pastry shell filled with creamed sweetbreads and mushrooms
les **crudités variées** lay krew·dee·tay vah·reeyay	assorted vegetables in a vinaigrette dressing
les **escargots** lay zehs·kahr·goh	snails
le **foie gras** luh fwah grah	fresh goose liver
le **pâté** luh pah·tay	liver purée
les **quenelles** lay kuh·nehl	light dumplings made of fish, fowl or meat, in cream sauce

With/Without...	**Avec/Sans...** ah·vehk/sawN...
I can't eat...	**Je ne peux pas manger...** zhuh nuh puh pah mawN·zhay...

les quenelles de brochet lay kuh·nehl duh broh·shay	dumplings made of pike in cream sauce
la quiche lah keesh	an open-faced egg and cheese tart filled with vegetables, meat or seafood
la quiche lorraine lah keesh loh·rayn	open-faced egg and cheese tart filled with bacon
les rillettes lay ree·yeht	pork mixture served as a spread for bread
la terrine lah teh·reen	pâté made from pork, poultry, game or fish
les toasts lay tohst	toasted pieces of bread with different toppings

Soup

l'aïgo boulido lah·ee·goh boolee·doh	garlic soup, a specialty of Provence
la bisque lah beesk	seafood stew
la bouillabaisse lah boo·yah·behs	seafood soup, a specialty of Marseilles
le consommé luh kohN·soh·may	clear soup
le consommé Célestine luh kohN·soh·may say·lehs·teen	clear soup with chicken and noodles
le consommé Colbert luh kohN·soh·may kohl·behr	clear soup with poached eggs, spring vegetables
le consommé à l'œuf luh kohN·soh·may ah luhf	clear soup with a raw egg

I'd like…	**Je voudrais…** zhuh voo·dray…
More…, please.	**Plus…, s'il vous plaît.** plews…seel voo play

le consommé au porto luh kohN·soh·may oh pohr·toh	clear soup with port wine
la garbure lah gahr·bewr	cabbage soup, often with pork or goose
le potage à l'ail luh poh·tahzh ah lie	garlic soup
le potage du barry luh poh·tahzh dew bah·ree	cream of cauliflower soup
le potage bilibi luh poh·tahzh bee·lee·bee	fish and oyster soup
le potage bonne ferme luh poh·tahzh bohn fehrm	soup with potatoes, leeks and sometimes bacon
le potage condé luh poh·tahzh kohN·day	soup with mashed red beans
le potage crécy luh poh·tahzh kray·see	soup with carrots and rice
le potage au cresson luh poh·tahzh oh kreh·sohN	watercress soup
le potage julienne luh poh·tahzh zhew·leeyehn	shredded vegetable soup
le potage Parmentier luh poh·tahzh pahr·mawN·teeyay	potato soup
le pot-au-feu luh poh-toh-fuh	meat and vegetable stew
le ragoût luh rah·goo	thick stew
la soupe à la bière lah soop ah lah beeyehr	beer soup with chicken stock and onions
la soupe aux choux lah soop oh shoo	cabbage soup
la soupe de haricots lah soop duh ah·ree·koh	bean soup

With/Without…	**Avec/Sans…** ah·vehk/sawN…
I can't eat…	**Je ne peux pas manger…** zhuh nuh puh pah mawN·zhay…

la soupe aux légumes lah soop oh lay·gewm — vegetable soup

la soupe à l'oignon lah soop ah loh·nyohN — French onion soup

la soupe au pistou lah soop oh pees·too — basil-vegetable soup, a specialty of Provence

la soupe de poulet lah soop duh poo·lay — chicken soup

la soupe de poisson lah soop duh pwah·sohN — soup with small fish, simmered and pureed

la soupe de tomates lah soop duh toh·maht — tomato soup

la soupe de volaille lah soop duh voh·lie — chicken soup

le velouté luh vuh·loo·tay — cream soup

Fish and Seafood

le anchois luh awN·shwah — anchovy

l'anguille lawN·geeyuh — eel

le bar luh bahr — bass

le bar aux herbes en chemise luh bah roh zayrb awN sheh·meez — bass stuffed with spinach and herbs, wrapped in lettuce and poached in white wine

le brochet luh broh·shay — pike

le calmar luh kahl·mahr — squid

les coquilles Saint-Jacques lay koh·keeyuh sehN·zhahk — breaded scallops sautéed in lemon juice and herbs

le crabe luh krahb — crab

la crevette lah kruh·veht — shrimp

la dorade lah doh·rahd — sea bass

I'd like…	**Je voudrais…** zhuh voo·dray…
More…, please.	**Plus…, s'il vous plaît.** plews…seel voo play

l'écrevisses lay·kruh·vees	crawfish
l'escargot lehs·kahr·goh	snail
l'espadon leh·spah·dohN	swordfish
le flétan luh flay·tawN	halibut
le hareng luh ah·rawN	herring
le homard luh oh·mahr	lobster
le homard cardinal luh oh·mahr kahr·dee·nahl	lobster cooked with mushrooms and truffles in a béchamel sauce
le huître luh wee·truh	oyster
la morue lah moh·rew	cod
la moule lah mool	mussel
les moules marinières lay mool mah·ree·neeyehr	mussels in white wine sauce
la palourde lah pah·loord	clam
le plateau de fruits de mer luh plah·toh duh frwee duh mehr	assorted seafood platter
le poulpe luh poolp	octopus
la sardine lah sahr·deen	sardine
le saumon luh soh·mohN	salmon
le saumon à l'oseille luh soh·mohN ah loh·zehy	salmon with sorrel sauce
la sole lah sohl	sole
le thon luh tohN	tuna
la truite lah trweet	trout

With/Without…	**Avec/Sans…** ah·vehk/sawN…
I can't eat…	**Je ne peux pas manger…** zhuh nuh puh pah mawN·zhay…

la truite aux amandes
lah trweet oh zah·mawNd

trout sautéed in a
creamy almond sauce

la truite meunière lah trweet muh·neeyehr

seasoned, breaded
trout, pan-fried in butter

Meat and Poultry

l'agneau lah·nyoh — lamb

le bacon luh beh·kohn — bacon

le bifteck luh beef·tehk — steak

le bœuf luh buhf — beef

la caille lah kie — quail

le canard luh kah·nahr — duck

le canard à l'orange
luh kah·nahr ah loh·rawNzh

duck braised with
orange liqueur

le cassoulet toulousain
luh kah·soo·lay too·loo·zehN

casserole of white
beans, mutton or salt
pork, sausage and
preserved goose

le cervela luh sehr·vuh·lah — garlic pork sausage

le chevreuil luh shuh·vruhy — venison

le cochon de lait luh koh·shohN duh lay — suckling pig

le coq au vin luh koh koh vehN

chicken in red wine
sauce

la côtelette de porc lah koh·tuh·leht duh pohr — pork chop

la dinde lah dehNd — turkey

l'épaule d'agneau farcie
lay·pohl dah·nyoh fahr·see

stuffed lamb shoulder

| I'd like… | **Je voudrais…** zhuh voo·dray… |
| More…, please. | **Plus…, s'il vous plaît.** plews…seel voo play |

76

l'escalope de veau normande lehs·kah·lohp duh voh nohr·mawNd	thinly sliced veal in cream sauce
l'escalope de veau milanaise lehs·kah·lohp duh voh mee·lah·nehz	thinly sliced veal in tomato sauce
le faisan luh fay·zawN	pheasant
le foie luh fwah	liver
le jambon luh zhawN·bohN	ham
le lapin luh lah·pehN	rabbit
le lapin à la Lorraine luh lah·pehN ah lah loh·rehn	rabbit in a mushroom cream sauce
le lapin à la moutarde luh lah·pehN ah lah moo·tahrd	rabbit in mustard sauce
les lardons lay lahr·dohN	cubes of salt pork
le porc luh pohr	pork
le poulet luh poo·lay	chicken
le poulet à l'estragon luh poo·lay ah lehs·trah·gohN	chicken in a tarragon cream sauce
le poulet chasseur luh poo·lay shah·suhr	chicken in a mushroom wine sauce
le ris luh rees	sweetbreads
la saucisse lah soh·sees	sausage
le steak luh stayk	steak
le tournedos luh toor·nuh·doh	small filet of beef
le veau luh voh	veal

rare	**saignant** say·nyawN
medium	**à point** ah pwehN
well-done	**bien cuit** beeyehN kwee

With/Without…	**Avec/Sans…** ah·vehk/sawN…
I can't eat…	**Je ne peux pas manger…** zhuh nuh puh pah mawN·zhay…

Vegetables and Staples

l'ail lie	garlic
l'artichaut lahr·tee·shoh	artichoke
les asperges lay zah·spehrzh	asparagus
l'aubergine loh·behr·zheen	eggplant [aubergine]
l'avocat lah·voh·kah	avocado
le brocoli luh broh·koh·lee	broccoli
la carotte lah kah·roht	carrot
les carottes vichy lay kah·roht vee·shee	carrots sauteed in butter
le céleri luh say·luh·ree	celery
le champignon luh shawN·pee·nyohN	mushroom
le chou luh shoo	cabbage
les choux verts à l'anglaise lay shoo vehr ah lawN·glehz	julienned cabbage, sautéed in butter
le chou-fleur luh shoo·fluhr	cauliflower
le chou-fleur au gratin luh shoo·fluhr oh grah·tehN	baked cauliflower, covered in cheese
la courgette lah koor·zheht	zucchini [courgette]
les épinards lay zay·pee·nahr	spinach
les épinards à la crème lay zay·pee·nahr ah lah krehm	creamed spinach
les haricots lay ah·ree·koh	beans
les haricots verts lay ah·ree·koh vehr	green beans

I'd like…	**Je voudrais…** zhuh voo·dray…
More…, please.	**Plus…, s'il vous plaît.** plews…seel voo play

la laitue lah lay·tew	lettuce
les légumes lay lay·gewm	vegetables
le maïs luh mah·ees	corn
l'oignon loh·nyohN	onion
l'olive loh·leev	olive
les pâtes lay paht	pasta
les petits pois lay puh·tee pwah	peas
le poivron *rouge/vert* luh pwah·vrohN *roozh/vehr*	*red/green* pepper
les poivrons farcis lay pwah·vrohN fahr·see	stuffed green peppers
la pomme de terre lah pohm duh tehr	potato

With/Without…	**Avec/Sans…** ah·vehk/sawN…
I can't eat…	**Je ne peux pas manger…** zhuh nuh puh pah mawN·zhay…

salade... sah·lahd...	salad...
– **antiboise** ahN·tee·bwahz	– with anchovy, green pepper, beets, rice and capers
– **niçoise** nee·swahz	– with tuna, anchovy, olives and vegetables
– **russe** rews	– with diced vegetables
– **de thon** duh tohN	– with tuna
– **verte** vehrt	– with mixed greens
le riz luh ree	rice
la tomate lah toh·maht	tomato

Fruit

l'abricot lah·bree·koh	apricot
l'ananas lah·nah·nah	pineapple
la banane lah bah·nahn	banana
le cassis luh kah·sees	black currant
la cerise lah suh·reez	cherry
le citron luh see·trohN	lemon
le citron vert luh see·trohN vehr	lime
la fraise lah frehz	strawberry
la framboise lah frawN·bwahz	raspberry
le fruit luh frwee	fruit
la groseille lah groh·zehy	red currant
le melon luh muh·lohN	melon

I'd like...	**Je voudrais...** zhuh voo·dray...
More..., please.	**Plus..., s'il vous plaît.** plews...seel voo play

la myrtille lah meer·teeyuh — blueberry

l'orange loh·rawNzh — orange

le pamplemousse luh pawN·pluh·moos — grapefruit

la pêche lah pehsh — peach

la poire lah pwahr — pear

la pomme lah pohm — apple

la prune lah prewn — plum

le raisin luh reh·zehN — grape

Cheese

le banon luh bah·nohN — mild goat's and cow's milk cheese with a nutty flavor

le bleu d'auvergne luh bluh doh·vehr·nyuh — cow's milk blue cheese with a strong flavor

le brie luh bree — soft cheese, ranging in strength and flavors

le camembert luh kah·mawN·behr — soft, raw cow's milk cheese

le coulommiers luh koo·luh·meeyay — soft, mild cow's milk cheese

la fondue lah fohN·dew — a pot of melted cheese dip

le fromage luh froh·mahzh — cheese

| With/Without… | Avec/Sans… ah·vehk/sawN… |
| I can't eat… | Je ne peux pas manger… zhuh nuh puh pah mawN·zhay… |

le fromage blanc luh froh·mahzh blawN — rich, creamy white cheese eaten for breakfast topped with cream and sugar

le fromage de chèvre luh froh·mahzh duh sheh·vruh — goat's milk cheese

le munster luh muhN·stuhr — soft, spicy cow's milk cheese from Alsace

le roquefort luh rohk·fohr — blue, soft and pungent sheep's milk cheese

le Saint-Paulin luh sehN·poh·lehN — smooth and mild cow's milk cheese

Dessert

la crêpe... lah krehp... — thin pancake...

– à la confiture ah lah kohN·fee·tewr — – with jam

– au sucre oh sew·kruh — – with sugar

– suzette sew·zeht — – in an orange-flavored sauce

le beignet luh beh·nyay — deep fried dough

le diplomate luh dee·ploh·maht — molded custard with fruit, lined with sponge cake that has been steeped in liqueur

le gâteau au fromage luh gah·toh oh froh·mahzh — cheesecake

| I'd like... | **Je voudrais...** zhuh voo·dray... |
| More..., please. | **Plus..., s'il vous plaît.** plews...seel voo play |

la génoise lah zhay·nwahz	sponge cake
le mont-blanc luh mohN·blawN	pastry with chestnut purée, whipped cream and meringue
la mousse au chocolat lah moos oh shoh·koh·lah	chocolate mousse
les petits fours lay puh·tee foor	bite-sized, decorated pastries
la poire belle-hélène lah pwahr behl·ehl·ehn	poached pears with ice cream and chocolate sauce
le sabayon luh sah·bah·yohN	creamy dessert made from egg yolks, wine, sugar and flavoring

With/Without…	**Avec/Sans…** ah·vehk/sawN…
I can't eat…	**Je ne peux pas manger…** zhuh nuh puh pah mawN·zhay…

la tarte aux fruits lah tahrt oh frwee	fruit pie or tart
la tarte tatin lah tahrt tah·tehN	upside down baked apple tart

Sauces and Flavorings

à la bonne femme ah lah bohn fehm	white wine sauce with vegetables
béarnaise beh·ahr·nehz	a sauce made with butter, eggs, shallots, wine and tarragon
bordelaise bohr·duh·lehz	sauce made with Bordeaux wine
chantilly shawN·tee·yee	sauce made with whipping cream
estragon eh·strah·gohN	with tarragon
florentine floh·rawN·teen	with spinach
hollandaise oh·lawN·dehz	creamy egg yolk and butter sauce
normande nohr·mawNd	fish sauce with shrimp or oysters
rémoulade ray·moo·lahd	mayonnaise mixed with mustard

I'd like…	**Je voudrais…** zhuh voo·dray…
More…, please.	**Plus…, s'il vous plaît.** plews…seel voo play
With/Without…	**Avec/Sans…** ah·vehk/sawN…
I can't eat…	**Je ne peux pas manger…** zhuh nuh puh pah mawN·zhay…

Drinks

Essential

The *wine list/drink menu*, please.	**La carte des *vins/boissons*, s'il vous plaît.** lah kahrt day *vehN/bwah•sohN* seel voo play
What do you recommend?	**Que me conseillez-vous?** kuh muh kohN•say•yay•voo
I'd like a *bottle/glass* of *red/white* wine.	**Je voudrais *une bouteille/un verre* de vin *rouge/blanc*.** zhuh voo•dray *ewn boo•tehy/uhN vehr* duh vehN *roozh/blawN*
The house wine, please.	**Le vin de la maison, s'il vous plaît.** luh vehN duh lah may•zohN seel voo play
Another *bottle/glass*, please.	***Une autre bouteille/Un autre verre*, s'il vous plaît.** *ewn oh•truh boo•tehy/uhN noh•truh vehr* seel voo play
I'd like a local beer.	**Je voudrais une bière locale.** zhuh voo•dray ewn beeyehr loh•kahl
Can I buy you a drink?	**Puis-je vous offrir un verre?** pwee•zhuh voo zoh•freer uhN vehr
Cheers!	**Santé!** sawN•tay
A *coffee/tea*, please.	**Un *café/thé*, s'il vous plaît.** uhN *kah•fay/tay* seel voo play
Black.	**Noir.** nwahr
With...	**Avec...** ah•vehk...
– milk	**– du lait** dew lay
– sugar	**– du sucre** dew sew•kruh
– artificial sweetener	**– de l'édulcorant** duh lay•dewl•koh•rawN

A..., please.	Un..., s'il vous plaît. uhN...seel voo play
– juice	– jus de fruit zhew duh frwee
– soda	– soda soh·dah
– (sparkling/still) water	– de l'eau (gazeuse/plate) duh loh (gah·zuhz/plaht)

Non-Alcoholic Drinks

le café luh kah·fay	coffee
le chocolat chaud luh shoh·koh·lah shoh	hot chocolate
la citronnade lah see·troh·nahd	lemonade
l'eau (gazeuse/plate) loh (gah·zuhz/plaht)	(sparkling/still) water
le jus de fruit luh zhew duh frwee	juice
le lait luh lay	milk
le soda luh soh·dah	soda
le thé (glacé) luh tay (glah·say)	(iced) tea

i

France offers a wide choice of mineral water. Popular French brands include Evian®, Vittel®, Volvic® and Badoit®; Perrier® and Vichy® are popular sparkling waters.

Café (espresso-style coffee) is also very popular. **Café** in France is not typically "to go." The French will enjoy their **café** while sitting with friends or just "people-watching." **Thé** (tea) is available and can be served **au lait** (with milk), **au citron** (with lemon), **à la menthe** (with mint leaves) or **glacé** (iced). **Tisane** (herbal tea) is also popular.

You May Hear...

Voulez-vous boire quelque chose?
voo·lay·voo bwahr kehl·kuh shohz

Can I get you a drink?

Avec du lait ou du sucre?
ah·vehk dew lay oo dew sew·kruh

With milk or sugar?

De l'eau gazeuse ou plate?
duh loh gah·zuhz oo plaht

Sparkling or still water?

Apéritifs, Cocktails and Liqueurs

le cognac luh koh·nyahk	brandy
le gin luh zheen	gin
le rhum luh ruhm	rum
le scotch luh skoh·tsh	scotch
la tequila lah teh·kee·lah	tequila
la vodka lah vohd·kah	vodka
le whisky luh wees·kee	whisky

Apéritifs are much more common than cocktails. Many are wine- and brandy-based with herbs and bitters; popular brands are Amer Picon®, Byrrh®, Dubonnet®, Pernod® and Ricard®.

Fruit-distilled brandies are popular as after-dinner drinks: **calvados** (apple), **kirsch** (cherry), **marc** (grape), **poire William** (pear) or **quetsche** (plum). Other popular liqueurs include the famous orange-flavored Grand Marnier® and Cointreau®.

Beer

la bière... lah beeyehr...   ...beer

– **en bouteille/pression**   – bottled/draft
awN boo·tehy/preh·seeyohN

– **brune/blonde** brewn/blohNd   – dark/light

– **blonde/pils** blohNd/peels   – lager/pilsener

– **locale/importée** loh·kahl/ehN·pohr·tay   – local/imported

– **non-alcoolisée** noh·nahl·koo·lee·zay   – non-alcoholic

Wine

le vin... luh vehN...   ...wine

– **rouge/blanc** roozh/blawN   – red/white

– **de maison/de table** duh may·zohN/duh   – house/table
tah·bluh

– **sec/sucré** sehk/sew·kray   – dry/sweet

– **pétillant** pay·tee·yawN   – sparkling

le champagne luh shawN·pah·nyuh   champagne

le vin de dessert luh vehN duh day·sehr   dessert wine

88

French wine is world-renowned. In restaurants, a **sommelier** (wine waiter) can offer advice on wine selections that will pair well with your meal—a tip is appreciated for this service.

You may want to sample some of the following:

Region	Main grape varieties	Popular wine styles
Alsace	Riesling, Pinot Blanc, Gewürztraminer	dry, semi-dry and sweet white wines
Bordeaux	Merlot, Cabernet-Sauvignon, Sémillon, Sauternes	full- and medium-bodied dry red wine; white dessert wine
Burgundy	Pinot Noir, Gamay, Chardonnay	full- and medium-bodied dry red wine; full-bodied dry white wine
Champagne	Chardonnay, Pinot Meunier, Pinot Noir	sparkling wine ranging from sweet to very dry
Côtes du Rhône	Grenache, Syrah, Viognier, Clairette	diverse red wine, from fruity to robust; full-bodied dry white wine
Languedoc-Roussillon	Carignan, Grenache, Mourvèdre, Cinsault, Merlot, Syrah	fine and table red wine; semi-dry and dry rosé wine; sweet white wine
Loire	Chenin Blanc, Sauvignon, Muscadet	lighter, dry and semi-dry white wine; some rosé and fruity red wine
Provence	Cinsault, Grenache, Mourvèdre, Syrah	dry and fruity rosé wine; full-bodied dry red wine; some white wine
Corsica	Nieluccio, Sciacarello, Vermentino,	dry rosé and red wine; light, dry white wine
Southwest France	Cabernet, Merlot, Sémillon, Sauvignon	full-bodied dry red wine; flavorful white wine

Menu Reader

les abats lay zah·bah	organ meat [offal]
les abattis lay zah·bah·tee	giblets
l'abricot lah·bree·koh	apricot
l'agneau lah·nyoh	lamb
l'ail lie	garlic
l'amande lah·mawNd	almond
l'ananas lah·nah·nah	pineapple
l'anchois lawN·shwah	anchovy
l'aneth lah·neht	dill
l'anguille lawN·gheeyuh	eel
l'artichaut lahr·tee·shoh	artichoke
l'asperge lah·spehrzh	asparagus

l'aubergine loh·buhr·zheen	eggplant [aubergine]
l'avocat lah·voh·kah	avocado
le babeurre luh bah·buhr	buttermilk
le bacon luh beh·kohN	bacon
la banane lah bah·nahn	banana
le bar luh bahr	bass
le basilic luh bah·see·leek	basil
la baudroie lah boh·drwah	monkfish
le beignet luh beh·nyay	fritter
la betterave lah beh·tuh·rahv	beet
le beurre luh buhr	butter
la bière lah beeyehr	beer
le bifteck d'aloyau luh beef·tehk dah·lwah·yoh	sirloin
le biscuit luh bees·kwee	cookie [biscuit]
le blé luh blay	wheat
le bleu luh bluh	blue cheese
le bœuf luh buhf	beef
les bonbons lay bohN·bohN	candy [sweets]
le boudin luh boo·dehN	blood sausage
le bouillon luh boo·yohN	broth
le cabillaud luh kah·beeyoh	haddock
la cacahuète lah kah·kah·weht	peanut
le café luh kah·fay	coffee
la caille lah kie	quail
le calmar luh kahl·mahr	squid
le canard luh kah·nahr	duck
la canneberge lah kah·nuh·behrzh	cranberry

la **cannelle** lah kah·nehl	cinnamon
la **câpre** lah kah·pruh	caper
le **caramel** luh kah·rah·mehl	caramel
la **carotte** lah kah·roht	carrot
le **cassis** luh kah·sees	black currant
le **céleri** luh say·luh·ree	celery
les **céréales** lay say·ray·ahl	cereal
la **cerise** lah suh·reez	cherry
la **chair de crabe** lah shehr duh krahb	crabmeat
le **champignon** luh shawN·pee·nyohN	mushroom
la **charcuterie** lah shar·kew·tuh·ree	cold cuts [charcuterie]
la **chèvre** lah sheh·vruh	goat
le **chevreau** luh shuh·vroh	kid (young goat)
la **chicorée** lah shee·koh·ray	chicory
les **chips** lay sheeps	potato chips [crisps]
le **chocolat** luh shoh·koh·lah	chocolate
le **chou** luh shoo	cabbage
le **chou rouge** luh shoo roozh	red cabbage
le **chou-fleur** luh shoo·fluhr	cauliflower
les **choux de Bruxelles** lay shoo duh brewk·sehl	Brussels sprouts
la **ciboule** lah see·bool	scallion [spring onion]
le **cidre** luh see·druh	cider
le **citron** luh see·trohN	lemon
le **citron vert** luh see·trohN vehr	lime
la **citrouille** lah see·truhy	pumpkin
les **cives** lay seev	chives
le **clou de girofle** luh kloo duh zhee·roh·fluh	clove

le cœur luh kuhr	heart
le cognac luh koh·nyahk	brandy
le colin luh koh·lehN	hake
la compote lah kohN·poht	stewed fruit
le concombre luh kohN·kohN·bruh	cucumber
la confiture lah kohN·fee·tewr	jam
les coquillages lay koh·kee·yahzh	shellfish
les coquilles lay koh·keeyuh	scallops
la coriandre lah koh·reeyawN·druh	cilantro [coriander]
le cornichon luh kohr·nee·shohN	gherkin/pickle
la côtelette lah koh·teh·leht	chop
la courgette lah koor·zheht	zucchini [courgette]
le crabe luh krahb	crab
la crème lah krehm	cream
la crème aigre lah krehm eh·gruh	sour cream
la crème anglaise lah krehm awN·glehz	custard
la crème fouettée lah krehm fooweh·tay	cream, whipped
la crème fraîche lah krehm frehsh	heavy cream
le crêpe luh krehp	pancake
le cresson luh kruh·sohN	watercress
la crevette lah kruh·veht	shrimp/prawn
le croissant luh krwah·sawN	croissant
le cumin luh kew·mehN	cumin
le cumin de près luh kew·mehN duh preh	caraway
la datte lah daht	date
la dinde lah dehNd	turkey
la dorade lah doh·rahd	sea bass

l'eau loh	water
l'eau tonique loh toh·neek	tonic water
l'échalote lay·shah·loht	shallot
l'edulcorant lay·dewl·koh·rawN	artificial sweetener
l'endive lawN·deev	endive
l'épaule lay·pohl	shoulder
les épices lay zay·pees	spices
les épinards lay zay·pee·nahr	spinach
l'escalope (de poulet) lehs·kah·lohp (duh poo·lay)	breast (of chicken)
l'escargot lehs·kahr·goh	snail
la écrevisse lah zay·kruh·vees	crayfish
l'espadon lehs·pah·dohN	swordfish
l'estragon lehs·trah·gohN	tarragon
le faisan luh feh·zawN	pheasant
le fenouil luh fuh·noohy	fennel
la feuille de laurier lah fuhy duh loh·reeyay	bay leaf
la figue lah feeg	fig
le filet luh fee·lay	loin
les fines herbes lay feen zayrb	herbs
les flageolets lay flah·zheh·lay	bean sprouts
le flétan luh flay·tawN	halibut
le foie luh fwah	liver
la fraise lah frehz	strawberry
la framboise lah frawN·bwahz	raspberry
les frites lay freet	French fries
le fromage luh froh·mahzh	cheese
le fromage blanc luh froh·mahzh blawN	soft, creamy cheese

le fromage de chèvre luh froh·mahzh duh sheh·vruh	goat cheese
le fromage frais luh froh·mahzh fray	soft, new cheese
le fruit luh frwee	fruit
les fruits de mer lay frwee duh mehr	seafood
le gâteau luh gah·toh	cake
le gâteau sec luh gah·toh sehk	cracker
la gaufre lah goh·fruh	waffle
la gelée lah zhuh·lay	jelly
le gibier luh zhee·beeyay	game
le gigot luh zhee·goh	leg
le gin luh zheen	gin
le gingembre luh zhehN·zhawN·bruh	ginger
la glace lah glahs	ice cream
le glaçon luh glah·sohN	ice (cube)
les gombos lay gohN·boh	okra
le goûter luh goo·tay	snack
la goyave lah goh·yahv	guava
la grenade lah gruh·nahd	pomegranate
la groseille lah groh·zehy	red currant
le hamburger luh awN·bewr·gayr	hamburger
le hareng luh ah·rawN	herring
les haricots lay ah·ree·koh	beans
les haricots verts lay ah·ree·koh vehr	green beans
le homard luh oh·mahr	lobster
le hot dog luh oht dohg	hot dog
l'huile d'olive lweel doh·leev	olive oil
l'huître lwee·truh	oyster

95

le jambon luh zhawN·bohN	ham
le _jaune/blanc_ d'œuf luh _zhohn/blawN_ duhf	egg _yolk/white_
le jus luh zhew	juice
le ketchup luh keht·shuhp	ketchup
le kiwi luh kee·wee	kiwi
le lait luh lay	milk
le lait de soja luh lait duh soh·zhah	soymilk [soya milk]
la laitue lah lay·tew	lettuce
la langue lah lawNg	tongue
le lapin luh lah·pehN	rabbit
les légumes lay lay·gewm	vegetables
la lentille lah lawN·tee·yuh	lentil
la limonade lah lee·moh·nahd	lemon soda
la liqueur d'oranges lah lee·kuhr doh·rawNzh	orange liqueur
la liqueur lah lee·kuhr	liqueur
les macaronis lay mah·kah·roh·nee	macaroni
le maïs luh mah·ees	sweet corn
la mandarine lah mawN·dah·reen	tangerine
la mangue lah mawNg	mango
le maquereau luh mah·kuh·roh	mackerel
la margarine lah mahr·gah·reen	margarine
la marmelade lah mahr·muh·lahd	marmalade
le marron luh mah·rohN	chestnut
la mayonnaise lah mah·yohN·nehz	mayonnaise
le melon luh muh·lohN	melon
la menthe lah mawNt	mint
la meringue lah muh·rehNg	meringue

le miel luh meeyehl	honey
la morue lah moh·rew	cod
les moules lay mool	mussels
la moutarde lah moo·tahrd	mustard
le mouton luh moo·tohN	mutton
la mûre lah mewr	blackberry
la myrtille lah meer·teeyuh	blueberry
le navet luh nah·vay	turnip
la noisette lah nwah·zeht	hazelnut
les noix lay nwah	nuts
la noix de cajou lah nwah duh kah·zhoo	cashew
la noix de coco lah nwah duh koh·koh	coconut
la noix de muscade lah nwah duh mew·skahd	nutmeg
la noix de pecan lah nwah duh peh·kawN	pecan
la nouille lah noohy	noodle
l'œuf luh	egg
l'oie lwah	goose
l'oignon loh·neeyohN	onion
l'olive loh·leev	olive
l'omelette loh·muh·leht	omelet
l'orange loh·rawNzh	orange
l'orangeade loh·rawN·zhayd	orange soda [squash]
l'origan loh·ree·gawN	oregano
le pain luh pehN	bread
le pain grillé luh pehN gree·yay	toast
les palourdes lay pah·loord	clams
le pamplemousse luh pawN·pluh·moos	grapefruit

le panais luh pah·nay	parsnip
la papaye lah pah·pie	papaya
la pastèque lah pahs·tehk	watermelon
la patate douce lah pah·taht doos	sweet potato
la pâte d'amande lah paht dah·mawNd	marzipan
le pâté luh pah·tay	pâté
les pâtes lay paht	pasta
les pâtisseries lay pah·tee·suh·ree	pastries
la pêche lah pehsh	peach
la perche lah pehrsh	sea perch
le persil luh pehr·seel	parsley
le petit pain luh puh·tee pehN	roll
les petits pois lay puh·tee pwah	peas
la pintade lah pehN·tahd	guinea fowl
la pizza lah peed·zah	pizza
les pois chiches lay pwah sheesh	chickpeas
la poire lah pwahr	pear
le poireaux luh pwah·roh	leek
le poisson luh pwah·sohN	fish
le poivre luh pwah·vruh	black pepper
le piment luh pee·mawN	chili pepper
le poivron luh pwah·vrohN	pepper (vegetable)
le piment doux luh pee·mawN doo	sweet pepper
la pomme lah pohm	apple
la pomme de terre lah pohm duh tehr	potato
le porc luh pohr	pork
le porto luh pohr·toh	port

le potage luh poh·tahzh	stew
la poule lah pool	hen
le poulet luh poo·lay	chicken
le poulpe luh poolp	octopus
la prune lah prewn	plum
le pruneau luh prew·noh	prune
la queue de bœuf lah kuh duh buhf	oxtail
le radis luh rah·dee	radish
le raisin luh reh·zehN	grape
le raisin sec luh reh·zehN sehk	raisin
la rhubarbe lah rew·bahrb	rhubarb
le rhum luh ruhm	rum
le riz luh ree	rice
le rognon luh roh·nyohN	kidney
le romarin luh roh·mah·rehN	rosemary
le rôti luh roh·tee	roast
le rôti de bœuf luh roh·tee duh buhf	roast beef
le safran luh sah·frawN	saffron
la salade lah sah·lahd	salad
le sandwich luh sawN·dweesh	sandwich
la sardine lah sahr·deen	sardine
la sauce lah sohs	sauce
la sauce à l'ail lah sohs ah lie	garlic sauce
la sauce aigre douce lah sohs eh·gruh doos	sweet and sour sauce
la sauce piquante lah sohs pee·kawNt	hot pepper sauce
la sauce soja lah sohs soh·zhah	soy sauce
la saucisse lah soh·sees	sausage

le saucisson luh soh·see·sohN	salami
la sauge lah sohzh	sage
le saumon luh soh·mohN	salmon
la scarole lah skah·rohl	escarole [chicory]
le scotch luh skoh·tsh	scotch
le sel luh sehl	salt
le sherry luh sheh·ree	sherry
le sirop luh see·rohp	syrup
le soda luh soh·dah	soda
le soja luh soh·zhah	soy [soya]/soybean [soya bean]
la sole lah sohl	sole
la soupe lah soop	soup
les spaghettis lay spah·geh·tee	spaghetti
les spiritueux lay spee·ree·tewuh	spirits
le steak luh stayk	steak
le sucre luh sew·kruh	sugar
les sucreries lay sew·kreh·ree	sweets
la tarte lah tahrt	pie
le thé luh tay	tea
le thon luh tohN	tuna
le thym luh tehN	thyme
le tofu luh toh·few	tofu
la tomate lah toh·maht	tomato
les tripes lay treep	tripe
la truffe lah trewf	truffle
la truite lah trweet	trout
la vanille lah vah·neeyuh	vanilla

le veau luh voh — veal

la venaison lah vuh·neh·sohN — venison

le vermouth luh vehr·moot — vermouth

la viande lah veeyawNd — meat

le vin luh vehN — wine

le vin de dessert luh vehN duh day·sehr — dessert wine

le vinaigre luh vee·neh·gruh — vinegar

la vodka lah vohd·kah — vodka

la volaille lah voh·lie — poultry

le whisky luh wees·kee — whisky

le yaourt luh yah·oort — yogurt

▼ *People*

Talking

Essential

Hello!/Hi!	**Bonjour!/Salut!** bohN·zhoor/sah·lew
How are you?	**Comment allez-vous?** koh·mawN tah·lay·voo
Fine, thanks.	**Bien, merci.** beeyehN mehr·see
Excuse me!	**Excusez-moi!** ehk·skew·zay·mwah
Do you speak English?	**Parlez-vous anglais?** pahr·lay·voo zawN·glay
What's your name?	**Comment vous appelez-vous?** koh·mawN voo zah·puh·lay·voo
My name is...	**Je m'appelle...** zhuh mah·pehl...
Nice to meet you.	**Enchanté♂/Enchantée♀.** awN·shawN·tay
Where are you from?	**D'où êtes-vous?** doo eht·voo
I'm from the U.K./U.S.	**Je viens** *du Royaume-Uni/des États-Unis.* zhuh veeyehN *dew rwah·yohm·ew·nee/day zay·tah·zew·nee*
What do you do for a living?	**Que faites-vous dans la vie?** kuh feht·voo dawN lah vee
I work for...	**Je travaille pour...** zhuh trah·vie poor...
I'm a student.	**Je suis étudiant♂/étudiante♀.** zhuh swee zay·tew·deeyawN♂/zay·tew·deeyawnt♀
I'm retired.	**Je suis à la retraite.** zhuh swee zah lah ruh·trayt
Do you like...?	**Aimez-vous...?** eh·may·voo...
Goodbye.	**Au revôir.** oh ruh·vwahr
See you later.	**À bientôt.** ah beeyehN·toh

i

When addressing someone, it is polite to include a title: **monsieur** for a man or **madame** for a woman, even if you suspect she is not married. **Mademoiselle** is used only when addressing young girls.

Communication Difficulties

Do you speak English?	**Parlez-vous anglais?** pahr·lay·voo zawN·glay
Does anyone here speak English?	**Est-ce que quelqu'un parle anglais ici?** ehs kuh kehl·kuhN pahrl awN·glay ee·see
I don't speak (much) French.	**Je ne parle pas (bien le) français.** zhuh nuh pahrl pah (beeyehN luh) frawN·say
Can you speak more slowly?	**Pouvez-vous parler plus lentement?** poo·vay·voo pahr·lay plew lawN·tuh·mawN
Can you repeat that?	**Pouvez-vous répéter?** poo·vay·voo ray·pay·tay
Excuse me?	**Excusez-moi?** ehk·skew·zay·mwah
Can you spell it?	**Pouvez-vous l'épeler?** poo·vay·voo lay·puh·lay
Please write it down.	**S'il vous plaît, écrivez-le.** seel voo play ay·kree·vay·luh
Can you translate this into English for me?	**Pouvez-vous traduire ceci en anglais pour moi?** poo·vay·voo trah·dweer suh·see awN nawN·glay poor mwah
What does *this/that* mean?	**Qu'est ce que *ceci/cela* veut dire?** kehs kuh *suh·see/suh·lah* vuh deer
I understand.	**Je comprends.** zhuh kohN·prawN
I don't understand.	**Je ne comprends pas.** zhuh nuh kohN·prawN pah
Do you understand?	**Comprenez-vous?** kohN·pruh·nay·voo

You May Hear...

Je parle un peu anglais.
zhuh pahrl uhN puh awN·glay

I only speak a little English.

Je ne parle pas anglais.
zhuh nuh pahrl pah zawN·glay

I don't speak English.

Making Friends

Hello!	**Bonjour!** bohN·zhoor
Good afternoon.	**Bon après-midi.** bohN nah·pray·mee·dee
Good evening.	**Bonsoir.** bohN·swahr
My name is...	**Je m'appelle...** zhuh mah·pehl...
What's your name?	**Comment vous appelez-vous?** koh·mawN voo zah·puh·lay·voo
I'd like to introduce you to...	**Je voudrais vous présenter...** zhuh voo·dray voo pray·zawN·tay...
Pleased to meet you.	**Enchanté♂/Enchantée♀.** awN·shawN·tay
How are you?	**Comment allez-vous?** koh·mawN tah·lay·voo
Fine, thanks. And you?	**Bien, merci. Et vous?** beeyehN mehr·see ay voo

i

In France, people greet each other with a firm handshake on first meeting. Once they become more familiar, people give from one to four or more kisses (cheek-to-cheek contact). Cheek-kissing among men, however, is usually reserved for family members and close friends.

Travel Talk

I'm here…	**Je suis ici…** zhuh swee zee·see…
– on business	– **pour les affaires** poor lay zah·fehr
– on vacation [holiday]	– **en vacances** awN vah·kawNs
– studying	– **pour étudier** poor ay·tew·deeyay
I'm staying for…	**Je reste pour…** zhuh rehst poor…
I've been here…	**Je suis ici pour…** zhuh swee zee·see poor…
– a day	– **un jour** uhN zhoor
– a week	– **une semaine** ewn suh·mehN
– a month	– **un mois** uhN mwah

▶ For numbers, see page 173.

| Where are you from? | **D'où êtes-vous?** doo eht·voo |
| I'm from… | **Je suis de…** zhuh swee duh… |

Relationships

Who are you with?	**Avec qui êtes-vous?** ah·vehk kee eht·voo
I'm here alone.	**Je suis seul**♂**/seule**♀. zhuh swee suhl
I'm with…	**Je suis avec…** zhuh swee zah·vehk…
– my husband/wife	– **mon mari**♂**/ma femme**♀ mohN mah·ree♂/mah fahm♀
– my boyfriend/ girlfriend	– **mon petit-ami**♂**/ma petite-amie**♀ mawN puh·tee·tah·mee♂/mah puh·tee·tah·mee♀

– a friend	– **un ami**♂/**une amie**♀ uhN nah•mee♂/ewn ah•mee♀
– friends	– **des amis** day zah•mee
– a colleague	– **un collègue**♂/**une collègue**♀ uhN koh•lehg♂/ewn koh•lehg♀
– colleagues	– **des collègues** day koh•lehg
When's your birthday?	**Quand est votre anniversaire?** kawN teh voh•truh ah•nee•vehr•sehr
How old are you?	**Quel âge avez-vous?** keh lahzh ah•vay•voo
I'm…	**J'ai…ans.** zhay…awN

▶ For numbers, see page 173.

Are you married?	**Êtes-vous marié**♂/**mariée**♀**?** eht•voo mah•reeyay
I'm…	**Je suis…** zhuh swee…
– single/in a relationship	– **célibataire/en ménage** say•lee•bah•tehr/ awN may•nahzh
– engaged	– **fiancé**♂/**fiancée**♀ feeyawN•say
– married	– **marié**♂/**mariée**♀ mah•reeyay
– divorced	– **divorcé**♂/**divorcée**♀ dee•vohr•say
– separated	– **séparé**♂/**séparée**♀ say•pah•ray
– widowed	– **veuf**♂/**veuve**♀ vuhf♂/vuhv♀
Do you have *children/ grandchildren*?	**Avez-vous des *enfants/petits-enfants*?** ah•vay•voo day *zawN•fawN/ puh•tee•zawN•fawN*

Work and School

What do you do for a living?	**Que faites-vous dans la vie?** kuh feht•voo dawN lah vee
What are you studying?	**Qu'étudiez-vous?** kay•tew•deeyay•voo
I'm studying French.	**J'étudie le français.** zhay•tew•dee luh frawN•say

I...	**Je...** zhuh...
– work *full-/part*-time	– **travaille à temps *plein/partiel*** trah·vie ah tawN *plehN/pahr·syehl*
– am unemployed	– **suis au chômage** swee zoh shoh·mahzh
– work at home	– **travaille à la maison** trah·vie ah lah may·zohN
Who do you work for?	**Pour qui travaillez-vous?** poor kee trah·vie·yay·voo
I work for...	**Je travaille pour...** zhuh trah·vie poor...
Here's my business card.	**Voici ma carte de visite.** vwah·see mah kahrt duh vee·zeet

▶ For business travel, see page 145.

Weather

What's the forecast?	**Que dit la météo?** kuh dee lah may·tay·oh
What *beautiful/ terrible* weather!	**Quel *beau/terrible* temps!** kehl *boh/ teh·ree·bluh* tawN
It's...	**Le temps est...** luh tawN ay...
– cool/warm	– **frais/chaud** fray/shoh
– cold/hot	– **froid/très chaud** frwah/tray shoh
– rainy/sunny	– **pluvieux/ensoleillé** plew·veeyuh/ awN·soh·lehyay
– snowy/icy	– **enneigé/gelé** awN·neh·zhay/zheh·lay
Do I need *a jacket/an umbrella*?	**Ai-je besoin *d'une veste/d'un parapluie*?** ay·zhuh buh·zwehN *dewn vehst/duhN pah·rah·plewee*

▶ For temperature, see page 180.

Romance

Essential

Would you like to go out for *a drink/dinner*?	**Voudriez-vous sortir *prendre un verre/ aller dîner*?** voo·dreeyay·voo sohr·teer *prawN·druh uhN vehr/ah·lay dee·nay*
What are your plans for *tonight/ tomorrow*?	**Quels sont vos projets pour *ce soir/ demain*?** kehl sohN voh proh·zhay poor *suh swahr/duh·mehN*
Can I have your (phone) number?	**Puis-je avoir votre numéro (de téléphone)?** pwee·zhuh ah·vwahr voh·truh new·may·roh (duh tay·lay·fohn)
Can I join you?	**Puis-je me joindre à vous?** pwee·zhuh muh zhwehN·druh ah voo
Can I buy you a drink?	**Puis-je vous offrir un verre?** pwee·zhuh voo zoh·freer uhN vehr
I love you.	**Je t'aime.** zhuh tehm

Making Plans

Would you like to go out…?	**Voudriez-vous sortir…?** voo·dreeyay·voo sohr·teer…
– for coffee	**– prendre un café** prawN·druh uhN kah·fay
– for a drink	**– prendre un verre** prawN·druh uhN vehr
– to dinner	**– aller dîner** ah·lay dee·nay
What are your plans for…?	**Quels sont vos projets pour…?** kehl sohN voh proh·zhay poor…
– today	**– aujourd'hui** oh·zhoor·dwee
– tonight	**– ce soir** suh swahr
– tomorrow	**– demain** duh·mehN
– this weekend	**– ce weekend** suh wee·kehnd

Where would you like to go?	**Où voudriez-vous aller?** oo voo·dreeyay·voo ah·lay
I'd like to go to…	**Je voudrais aller à…** zhuh voo·dray ah·lay ah…
Do you like…?	**Aimez-vous…?** eh·may·voo…
Can I have your *phone number/ e-mail*?	**Puis-je avoir votre *numero de téléphone/ mail*?** pwee·zhuh ah·vwahr voh·truh *new·may·roh duh tay·lay·fohn/mehyl*

▶ For e-mail and phone, see page 49.

Pick-up [Chat-up] Lines

Can I join you?	**Puis-je me joindre à vous?** pwee·zhuh muh zhwehN·druh ah voo
You're very attractive.	**Vous êtes très beau ♂/belle ♀.** voo zeht tray boh ♂/behl ♀
Let's go somewhere quieter.	**Allons dans un endroit plus calme.** ah·lohN dawN uhN nawN·drwah plew kahlm

Accepting and Rejecting

| I'd love to. | **Avec plaisir.** ah·vehk play·zeer |
| Where should we meet? | **Où devons-nous nous retrouver?** oo duh·vohN·noo noo ruh·troo·vay |

I'll meet you at *the bar/your hotel*.	**Je vous retrouverai *au bar/à votre hôtel*.** zhuh voo ruh·troo·vuh·ray *oh bahr/ah voh·truh oh·tehl*
I'll come by at…	**Je viendrai à…** zhuh veeyehN·dray ah…

▶ For time, see page 175.

I'm busy.	**Je suis occupé♂/occupée♀.** zhuh swee zoh·kew·pay
I'm not interested.	**Je ne suis pas intéressé♂/intéressée♀.** zhuh nuh swee pah ehN·tay·reh·say
Leave me alone.	**Laissez-moi tranquille.** leh·say mwah trawN·keel
Stop bothering me!	**Fichez-moi la paix!** fee·shay·mwah lah pay

Getting Physical

Can I *hug/kiss* you?	**Puis-je vous *enlacer/embrasser*?** pwee·zhuh voo *zawN·lah·say/zawN·brah·say*
Yes.	**Oui.** wee
No.	**Non.** nohN
Stop!	**Arrêtez!** ah·reh·tay
I love you.	**Je t'aime.** zhuh tehm

Sexual Preferences

Are you gay?	**Êtes-vous gay?** eht·voo gay
I'm…	**Je suis…** zhuh swee…
– heterosexual	– **hétérosexuel♂/hétérosexuelle♀** ay·tay·roh·sehk·sewehl
– homosexual	– **homosexuel♂/homosexuelle♀** oh·moh·sehk·sewehl
– bisexual	– **bisexuel♂/bisexuelle♀** bee·sehk·sewehl
Do you like *men/women*?	**Aimez-vous les *hommes/femmes*?** ay·may·voo lay *zohm/fahm*

▼ Fun

Sightseeing

Essential

Where's the tourist information office?	**Où est l'office de tourisme?** oo ay loh·fees duh too·ree·smuh
What are the main sights?	**Quelles sont les choses importantes à voir?** kehl sohN lay shoh zehN·pohr·tawN tah vwahr
Do you offer tours in English?	**Proposez-vous des visites en anglais?** Proh·poh·zay·voo day vee·zeet zawN nawN·glay
Can I have a *map/guide*?	**Puis-je avoir *une carte/un guide*?** pwee·zhuh ah·vwahr *ewn kahrt/uhN geed*

Tourist Information Office

Do you have information on...?	**Avez-vous des renseignements sur...?** ah·vay·voo day rawN·seh·nyuh·mawN sewr...
Can you recommend...?	**Pouvez-vous me conseiller...?** poo·vay·voo muh kohN·say·yay...
– a bus tour	**– une visite en bus** ewn vee·zeet awN bews
– an excursion to...	**– une excursion pour...** ewn ehk·skewr·seeyohN poor...
– a tour of...	**– une visite de...** ewn vee·zeet duh...

Offices de tourisme or **syndicats d'initiative** (tourism offices) are usually located near the downtown area, next to train stations or close to city hall. They can provide a wealth of information about lodging, entertainment, restaurants, etc.

Tours

I'd like to go on the excursion to…	**Je voudrais faire cette excursion à…** zhuh voo·dray fehr seh tehk·skewr·seeyohN nah…
When's the next tour?	**Quand a lieu la prochaine visite?** kawN tah leeyuh lah proh·shehn vee·zeet
Are there tours in English?	**Y-a-t-il des visites en anglais?** yah·teel day vee·zeet zawN nawN·glay
Is there an English *guide book/audio guide*?	**Y-a-t-il un *guide/audio guide* en anglais?** yah·teel uhN *geed/oh·deeyoh geed* awN nawN·glay
What time do we *leave/return*?	**À quelle heure *partons-nous/ revenons-nous*?** ah keh luhr *pahr·tohN·noo/ ruh·vuh·nohN-noo*
We'd like to see…	**Nous voudrions voir…** noo voo·dreeyohN vwahr…
Can we stop here…?	**Pouvons-nous nous arrêter ici pour…?** poo·vohN·noo noo zah·reh·tay ee·see poor…
– to take photos	**– prendre des photos** prawN·druh day foh·toh
– for souvenirs	**– acheter des souvenirs** ah·shtay day soo·vuh·neer
– for the restrooms [toilets]	**– aller aux toilettes** ah·lay zoh twah·leht
Is it handicapped [disabled]-accessible?	**Est-ce que c'est accessible aux handicapés?** ehs kuh say tahk·say·see·bluh oh zawN·dee·kah·pay

▶ For ticketing, see page 19.

Sights

Where's…?	**Où est…?** oo ay…
– the battleground	– **le champ de bataille** luh shawN duh bah·tie
– the botanical garden	– **le jardin botanique** luh zhahr·dehN boh·tah·neek
– the castle	– **le château** luh shah·toh
– the downtown area	– **le centre-ville** luh sawN·truh·veel
– the fountain	– **la fontaine** lah fohN·tehn
– the library	– **la bibliothèque** lah bee·bleeyoh·tehk
– the market	– **le marché** luh mahr·shay
– the museum	– **le musée** luh mew·zay
– the old town	– **la vieille ville** lah veeyeh·yuh veel
– the opera house	– **l'opéra** loh·pay·rah
– the palace	– **le palais** luh pah·lay
– the park	– **le parc** luh pahrk
– the ruins	– **les ruines** lay rween
– the shopping area	– **le quartier commercial** luh kahr·teeyay koh·mehr·seeyahl
– the town square	– **la grand-place** lah grawN·plahs
Can you show me on the map?	**Pouvez-vous me montrer sur la carte?** poo·vay-voo muh mohN·tray sewr lah kahrt

▶ For directions, see page 34.

Impressions

It's...	C'est... say...
– amazing	– **surprenant** sewr·preh·nawN
– beautiful	– **beau** boh
– boring	– **ennuyeux** awN·nwee·yuh
– interesting	– **intéressant** ehN·tay·reh·sawN
– magnificent	– **magnifique** mah·nee·feek
– romantic	– **romantique** roh·mawN·teek
– strange	– **étrange** ay·trawNzh
– terrible	– **terrible** teh·ree·bluh
– ugly	– **laid** lay
I (don't) like it.	**Je (n')aime (pas).** zhuh (n)ehm (pah)

Religion

Where's...?	Où est...? oo ay...
– the cathedral	– **la cathédrale** lah kah·tay·drahl
– the *Catholic/Protestant* church	– **l'église *catholique/protestante*** lay·gleez *kah·toh·leek/proh·tehs·tawNt*

– the mosque	– **la mosquée** lah mohs·kay
– the shrine	– **le lieu saint** luh leeyuh sehN
– the synagogue	– **la synagogue** lah see·nah·gohg
– the temple	– **le temple** luh tawN·pluh
What time is the service?	**À quelle heure est la messe?** ah keh luhr ay lah mehs

Shopping

Essential

Where's the *market/ mall [shopping centre]?*	**Où est le *marché/centre commercial*?** oo ay luh *mahr·shay/sawN·truh koh·mehr·seeyahl*
I'm just looking.	**Je regarde seulement.** zhuh ruh·gahrd suhl·mawN
Can you help me?	**Pouvez-vous m'aider?** poo·vay·voo meh·day
I'm being helped.	**On s'occupe de moi.** ohN soh·kewp duh mwah
How much?	**Combien ça coûte?** kohN·beeyehN sah koot
That one, please.	**Celui-ci♂/Celle-ci♀, s'il vous plaît.** suh·lwee·see♂/sehl see♀ seel voo play
That's all.	**C'est tout.** say too
Where can I pay?	**Où puis-je payer?** oo pwee·zhuh pay·yay
I'll pay *in cash/by credit card.*	**Je paierai *en espèces/par carte de crédit.*** zhuh pay·ray *awN neh·spehs/pahr kahrt duh kray·dee*
A receipt, please.	**Un reçu, s'il vous plaît.** uhN ruh·sew seel voo play

Stores

Where's...?   **Où est...** oo ay...

– the antiques store   – **l'antiquaire** lawN·tee·kehr

– the bakery   – **la boulangerie** lah boo·lawN·zhuh·ree

– the bank   – **la banque** lah bawNk

– the bookstore   – **la librairie** lah lee·breh·ree

– the clothing store   – **le magasin de vêtements** luh
                                  mah·gah·zehN duh veht·mawN

– the delicatessen   – **le charcuterie** luh shar·kew·tuh·ree

– the department   – **le grand magasin** luh grawN mah·gah·zehN
  store

– the gift shop   – **la boutique cadeaux** lah boo·teek kah·doh

– the health food   – **le magasin de diététique**
  store   luh mah·gah·zehN duh deeyay·tay·teek

– the jeweler   – **la bijouterie** lah bee·zhoo·tuh·ree

– the liquor store   – **le marchand de vins et de spiritueux** luh
  [off-licence]   mahr·shawN duh vehN ay duh spee·ree·tewuh

– the market   – **le marché** luh mahr·shay

– the music store	– **le disquaire** luh dees·kehr
– the pastry shop	– **la pâtisserie** lah pah·tee·suh·ree
– the pharmacy [chemist]	– **la pharmacie** lah fahr·mah·see
– the produce [grocery] store	– **le magasin de fruits et légumes** luh mah·gah·zehN duh frwee zay lay·gewm
– the shoe store	– **le magasin de chaussures** luh mah·gah·zehN duh shoh·sewr
– the shopping mall [shopping centre]	– **le centre commercial** luh sawN·truh koh·mehr·seeyahl
– the souvenir store	– **le magasin de souvenirs** luh mah·gah·zehN duh soo·vuh·neer
– the supermarket	– **le supermarché** luh sew·pehr·mahr·shay
– the tobacconist	– **le bureau de tabac** luh bew·roh duh tah·bahk
– the toy store	– **le magasin de jouets** luh mah·gah·zehN duh zhooway

Services

Can you recommend…?	**Pouvez-vous me conseiller…?** poo·vay·voo muh kohN·say·yay…
– a barber	– **un coiffeur pour hommes** uhN kwah·fuhr poor ohm
– a dry cleaner	– **une teinturerie** ewn tehN·tewr·ree
– a hairstylist	– **un coiffeur** uhN kwah·fuhr
– a laundromat [launderette]	– **une laverie automatique** ewn lah·vuh·ree oh·toh·mah·teek
– a nail salon	– **une onglerie** ewn ohN·gluh·ree
– a spa	– **une station de balnéothérapie** ewn stah·seeyohN duh bahl·nayoh·tay·rah·pee
– a travel agency	– **une agence de voyage** ewn ah·zhawNs duh vwah·yahzh

Can you...this?	**Pouvez-vous...ceci?** poo·vay·voo...suh·see
– alter	– **changer** shawN·zhay
– clean	– **nettoyer** neh·twah·yay
– fix [mend]	– **raccourcir** rah·koor·seer
– press	– **repasser** ruh·pah·say
When will it be ready?	**Quand cela sera-t-il prêt?** kawN suh·lah seh·rah·teel preh

Spa

I'd like...	**Je voudrais...** zhuh voo·dray...
– an *eyebrow/ bikini* wax	– **une épilation à la cire *des sourcils/du maillot*** ewn ay·pee·lah·seeyohN nah lah seer *day soor·seel/dew mieyoh*
– a facial	– **un soin du visage** uhN swehN dew vee·zahzh
– a *manicure/ pedicure*	– **une *manucure/pédicure*** ewn *mah·new·kewr/pay·dee·kewr*
– a (sports) massage	– **un massage (sportif)** uhN mah·sahzh (spohr·teef)
Do you offer...?	**Proposez-vous...?** proh·poh·zay·voo...
– acupuncture	– **de l'acupuncture** duh lah·kew·pohNk·tewr
– aromatherapy	– **de l'aromathérapie** duh lah·roh·mah·tay·rah·pee
– oxygen treatment	– **des soins à l'oxygène** day swehN ah lohk·see·zhehn
– a sauna	– **un sauna** uhN soh·nah

i **Les stations de balnéothérapie** (spas) are popular in France; day spas, especially, can be found in Paris and along the French Riviera. Many villages and resorts specialize in water therapies. The hot springs at Dax have been popular since Roman times, and the town is still one of France's most popular spa destinations. Some spas in the Bordeaux region specialize in wine-based therapies. In addition to the therapies, spa towns may also offer beautiful scenery, casinos, restaurants and outdoor activities.

Hair Salon

I'd like…	**Je voudrais…** zhuh voo·dray…
– an appointment for *today/tomorrow*	– **un rendez-vous pour *aujourd'hui/ demain*** uhN rawN·day·voo poor oh·zhoor·dwee/duh·mehN
– some color/ highlights	– **une couleur/des mèches** ewn koo·luhr/ day mehsh
– my hair styled/ blow-dried	– **une mise en forme/un brushing** ewn mee zawN fohrm/uhN bruh·sheeng
– a haircut	– **une coupe** ewn koop
A trim, please.	**Égalisez les pointes, s'il vous plaît.** ay·gah·lee·zay lay pwehN seel voo play
Not too short.	**Pas trop court.** pah troh koor
Shorter here.	**Plus court ici.** plew koor ee·see

Sales Help

When do you *open/close*?	**À quelle heure *ouvrez-vous/ fermez-vous*?** ah kehl uhr oo·vray·voo/fehr·may·voo

Where's...?	Où est...? oo ay...
– the cashier	– la caisse lah kehs
– the escalator	– l'escalator lehs·kah·lah·tohr
– the elevator [lift]	– l'ascenseur lah·sawN·suhr
– the fitting room	– la cabine d'essayage lah kah·been deh·say·yahzh
– the store directory	– le plan du magasin luh plawN dew mah·gah·zehN
Can you help me?	Pouvez-vous m'aider? poo·vay·voo meh·day
I'm just looking.	Je regarde seulement. zhuh ruh·gahrd suhl·mawN
I'm being helped.	On s'occupe de moi. ohN soh·kewp duh mwah
Do you have...?	Avez-vous...? ah·vay·voo...
Can you show me...?	Pouvez-vous me montrer...? poo·vay·voo muh mohN·tray...
Can you *ship/wrap* it?	Pouvez-vous *le livrer/l'emballer*? poo·vay·voo *luh lee·vray/lawN·bah·lay*
How much?	Combien ça coûte? kohN·beeyehN sah koot
That's all.	C'est tout. say too

▶ For clothing items, see page 129.

▶ For food items, see page 90.

▶ For souvenirs, see page 125.

You May Hear...

Je peux vous aider? zhuh puh voo zeh·day	Can I help you?
Un instant. uhN nehNs·tawN	One moment.
Que désirez-vous? kuh day·zee·ray·voo	What would you like?
Autre chose? oh·truh shohz	Anything else?

You May See...

OUVERT/FERMÉ	open/closed
FERMÉ POUR LE DÉJEUNER	closed for lunch
CABINE D'ESSAYAGE	fitting room
CAISSE	cashier
ESPÈCES SEULEMENT	cash only
CARTES ACCEPTÉES	credit cards accepted
HEURES D'OUVERTURE	business hours
SORTIE	exit

Preferences

I'd like something...	**Je voudrais quelque chose...** zhuh voo·dray kehl·kuh shohz...
– cheap/expensive	**– de bon marché/cher** duh bohN mahr·shay/shehr
– larger/smaller	**– de plus *grand/petit*** duh plew *grawN/puh·tee*
– from this region	**– de cette région** duh seht ray·zheeyohN
Around...euros.	**Pour à peu près...euros.** poor ah puh pray...uh·roh
Is it real?	**Est-ce que c'est du vrai?** ehs kuh say dew vray
Can you show me *this/that*?	**Pouvez-vous me montrer *ceci/cela*?** poo·vay-voo muh mohN·tray *suh·see/suh·lah*

Decisions

That's not quite what I want.	**Ce n'est pas exactement ce que je veux.** suh nay pah zehk·sahk·tuh·mawN suh kuh zhuh vuh
No, I don't like it.	**Non, je n'aime pas.** nohN zhuh nehm pah
It's too expensive.	**C'est trop cher.** say troh shehr

| I have to think about it. | **Je dois réfléchir.** zhuh dwah ray·flay·sheer |
| I'll take it. | **Je le♂/la♀ prends.** zhuh luh♂/lah♀ prawN |

Bargaining

That's too much.	**C'est beaucoup trop.** say boh·koo troh
I'll give you…	**Je vous en propose…** zhuh voo zawN proh·pohz…
I have only…euros.	**Je n'ai que…euros.** zhuh nay kuh…uh·roh
Is that your best price?	**Est-ce que c'est votre meilleur prix?** ehs kuh say voh·truh mehy·yuhr pree
Can you give me a discount?	**Pouvez-vous me faire une remise?** poo·vay-voo muh fehr ewn ruh·meez

▶ For numbers, see page 173.

Paying

How much?	**Combien ça fait?** kohN·beeyehN sah fay
I'll pay…	**Je paierai…** zhuh pay·ray…
– in cash	**– en espèces** awN nehs·pehs
– by credit card	**– par carte de crédit** pahr kahrt duh kray·dee
– by traveler's check [cheque]	**– avec des chèques de voyages** ah·vehk day shehk duh vwah·yahzh
A receipt, please.	**Un reçu, s'il vous plaît.** uhN ruh·sew seel voo play

i Cash (the euro) is always accepted. Credit and debit cards can be used in cash machines and for purchases. Check with your bank before leaving to obtain a PIN for both debit and credit cards; you'll usually be asked to enter your PIN instead of signing when making purchases. Traveler's checks are also widely accepted in France.

You May Hear...

Comment voulez-vous payer? koh·mawN voo·lay·voo pay·yay

How are you paying?

Votre carte de crédit est refusée. voh·truh kahrt duh kray·dee tay ruh·few·zay

Your credit card has been declined.

Une pièce d'identité, s'il vous plaît. ewn peeyehs dee·dawN·tee·tay seel voo play

ID, please.

Nous n'acceptons pas les cartes de crédit. noo nahk·sehp·tohN pah lay kahrt duh kray·dee

We don't accept credit cards.

En espèces seulement, s'il vous plaît. awN nehs·pehs suhl·mawN seel voo play

Cash only, please.

Complaints

I'd like...

Je voudrais... zhuh voo·dray...

– to exchange this

– échanger ceci ay·shawN·zhay suh·see

– a refund

– un remboursement uhN rawN·boor·suh·mawN

– to see the manager

– voir le responsable vwahr luh rehs·pohN·sah·bluh

Souvenirs

a bottle of wine

une bouteille de vin ewn boo·tehy duh vehN

a box of chocolates

une boîte de chocolats ewn bwaht duh shoh·koh·lah

some crystal

du cristal dew kree·stahl

a doll

une poupée ewn poo·pay

some jewelry

des bijoux day bee·zhoo

a key ring

un porte-clés uhN pohrt·klay

a postcard

une carte postale ewn kahrt pohs·tahl

some pottery	**des poteries** day poh·tuh·ree
a T-shirt	**un t-shirt** uhN tee·shuhrt
a toy	**un jouet** uhN zhooway
Can I see *this/that*?	**Puis-je voir *ceci/cela*?** pwee·zhuh vwahr *suh·see/suh·lah*
I'd like…	**Je voudrais…** zhuh voo·dray…
– a battery	**– une pile** ewn peel
– a bracelet	**– un bracelet** uhN brahs·lay
– a brooch	**– une broche** ewn brohsh
– a clock	**– une pendule** ewn pawN·dewl
– earrings	**– des boucles d'oreille** day boo·kluh doh·rehy
– a necklace	**– un collier** uhN koh·leeyay
– a ring	**– une bague** ewn bahg
– a watch	**– une montre** ewn mohN·truh

I'd like…	**Je voudrais…** zhuh voo·dray…
– copper	**– du cuivre** dew kwee·vruh
– crystal	**– du cristal** dew krees·tahl
– diamonds	**– des diamants** day deeyah·mawN
– *white/yellow* gold	**– de l'or** *blanc/jaune* duh lohr *blawN/zhohn*
– pearls	**– des perles** day pehrl
– pewter	**– de l'étain** duh lay·tehN
– platinum	**– du platine** dew plah·teen
– sterling silver	**– de l'argent fin** duh lahr·zhawN fehN
Is this real?	**Est-ce que c'est du vrai?** ehs kuh say dew vray
Can you engrave it?	**Pouvez-vous le graver?** poo·vay·voo luh grah·vay

France offers a wide array of souvenirs for the traveler. Souvenir shops are located throughout larger cities, especially near tourist destinations. Certain regions in France are known for their specialty items that make great souvenirs and gifts: lace from Alençon, crystal from Baccarat, perfume from Grasse, porcelain from Limoges and the latest fashions from Paris. Markets and specialty shops are great places to find these regional specialties.

i

France is well-known for its classic and cutting-edge jewelry design. Paris and the French Riviera are home to famous jewelry houses such as Boucheron®, Cartier® and VanCleef & Arpels®.

Antiques

How old is it?	**De quand date-t-il♂/date-elle♀?** duh kawN dah·teel♂/dah·tehl♀
Do you have anything from the…period?	**Avez-vous quelque chose de la période…?** ah·vay·voo kehl·kuh shohz duh lah pay·reeyohd…
Do I have to fill out any forms?	**Dois-je remplir des formulaires?** dwah·zhuh rawN·pleer day fohr·mew·lehr
Is there a certificate of authenticity?	**Y-a-t-il un certificat d'authenticité?** yah·teel uhN sehr·tee·fee·kah doh·tawN·tee·see·tay
Can you *ship/wrap* it?	**Pouvez-vous *le livrer/l'emballer*?** poo·vay·voo *luh lee·vray/lawN·bah·lay*

Clothing

I'd like…	**Je voudrais…** zhuh voo·dray…
Can I try this on?	**Puis-je essayer ceci?** pwee·zhuh eh·say·yay suh·see
It doesn't fit.	**Ça ne va pas.** sah nuh vah pah
It's too…	**C'est trop…** say troh…
– big/small	– **grand/petit** grawN/puh·tee
– short/long	– **court/long** koor/lohng
– tight/loose	– **serré/large** seh·ray/lahrzh

| Do you have this in size…? | **Avez-vous ceci en taille…?** ah·vay·voo suh·see awN tie… |
| Do you have this in a *bigger/smaller* size? | **Avez-vous ceci en plus *grand/petit*?** ah·vay·voo suh·see awN plew *grawN/puh·tee* |

▶ For numbers, see page 173.

You May Hear…

Ça vous va très bien. sah voo vah tray beeyehN	That looks great on you.
Comment ça me va? koh·mawN sah muh vah	How does it fit?
Nous n'avons pas votre taille. noo nah·vohN pah voh·truh tie	We don't have your size.

Haute couture (designer fashion) and **prêt-à-porter** (off-the-rack; literally, ready-to-wear) boutiques can be found throughout Paris. The latest fashions by Dior®, Givenchy®, Saint-Laurent®, Chanel®, Jean-Paul Gaultier®, Ungaro®, Feraud®, Yamamoto® and Hermès® can be found in Paris well before making it to the U.S. or the U.K. Airport boutiques offer tax-free shopping and may have cheaper prices but fewer selections.

You May See…

HOMMES	men's
FEMMES	women's
ENFANTS	children's

Color

I'd like something… **Je voudrais quelque chose de…** zhuh voo·dray kehl·kuh shohz duh…

– beige	**– beige** behzh
– black	**– noir** nwahr
– blue	**– bleu** bluh
– brown	**– marron** mah·rohN
– green	**– vert** vehr
– gray	**– gris** gree
– orange	**– orange** oh·rawNzh
– pink	**– rose** rohz
– purple	**– violet** veeyoh·lay
– red	**– rouge** roozh
– white	**– blanc** blawN
– yellow	**– jaune** zhohn

Clothes and Accessories

a backpack	**un sac à dos** uhN sahk ah doh
a belt	**une ceinture** ewn sehN·tewr
a bikini	**un bikini** uhN bee·kee·nee
a blouse	**un chemisier** uhN shuh·mee·zeeyay
a bra	**un soutien-gorge** uhN soo·teeyehN·gohrzh
briefs [underpants]/ panties	**des slips/des culottes** day sleep/day kew·loht
a coat	**un manteau** uhN mawN·toh
a dress	**une robe** ewn rohb
a hat	**un chapeau** uhN shah·poh
a jacket	**une veste** ewn vehst
jeans	**un jean** uhN zheen

pajamas	**un pyjama** uhN pee·zhah·mah
pants [trousers]	**un pantalon** uhN pawN·tah·lohN
pantyhose [tights]	**un collant** uhN koh·lawN
a purse [handbag]	**un sac à main** uhN sahk ah mehN
a raincoat	**un imperméable** uhN nehN·pehr·may·ah·bluh
a scarf	**une écharpe** ewn ay·sharp
a shirt	**une chemise** ewn shuh·meez
shorts	**un short** unN shohrt
a skirt	**une jupe** ewn zhewp
socks	**des chaussettes** day shoh·seht
a suit	**un costume** uhN kohs·tewm
sunglasses	**des lunettes** day lew·neht
a sweater	**un pull** uhN pewl
a sweatshirt	**un sweat-shirt** uhN sweht·shuhrt
a swimsuit	**un maillot de bain** uhN mie·yoh duh behN
a T-shirt	**un t-shirt** uhN tee·shuhrt
a tie	**une cravate** ewn krah·vaht
underwear	**un sous-vêtement** uhN soo·veht·mawN

Fabric

I'd like…	**Je voudrais…** zhuh voo·dray…
– cotton	**– du coton** dew koh·tohN
– denim	**– du jean** dew zheen
– lace	**– de la dentelle** duh lah dawN·tehl
– leather	**– du cuir** dew kweer
– linen	**– du lin** dew lehN
– silk	**– de la soie** duh lah swah
– wool	**– de la laine** duh lah lehn
Is it machine washable?	**Est-ce lavable en machine?** ehs lah·vah·bluh awN mah·sheen

Shoes

I'd like...	**Je voudrais...** zhuh voo·dray...
– high-heels/flats	**– des talons *hauts/plats*** day tah·lohN *oh/plah*
– boots	**– des bottes** day boht
– loafers	**– des mocassins** day moh·kah·sehN
– sandals	**– des sandales** day sawN·dahl
– shoes	**– des chaussures** day shoh·sewr
– slippers	**– des chaussons** day shoh·sohN
– sneakers	**– des tennis** day tay·nees
Size...	**Taille...** tie...

▶ For numbers, see page 173.

Sizes

small (S)	**petit** puh·tee
medium (M)	**moyen** mwah·yawN
large (L)	**grand** grawN
extra large (XL)	**très grand** tray grawN
petite	**menue** muh·new
plus size	**grande taille** grawNd tie

Newsstand and Tobacconist

Do you sell English-language newspapers?	**Vendez-vous des journaux en anglais?** vawN·day·voo day zhoor·noh awN nawN·glay
I'd like...	**Je voudrais...** zhuh voo·dray...
– candy [sweets]	**– des bonbons** day bohN·bohN
– chewing gum	**– du chewing gum** dew shew·weeng guhm
– a chocolate bar	**– une barre de chocolat** ewn bahr duh shoh·koh·lah
– a cigar	**– un cigare** uhN see·gahr

– a *pack/carton* of cigarettes	– **un pack/une cartouche de cigarettes** uhN pahk/ewn kahr·toosh duh see·gah·reht
– a lighter	– **un briquet** uhN bree·kay
– a magazine	– **un magazine** uhN mah·gah·zeen
– matches	– **des allumettes** day zah·lew·meht
– a newspaper	– **un journal** uhN zhoor·nahl
– a pen	– **un stylo** uhN stee·loh
– a postcard	– **une carte postale** ewn kahrt pohs·tahl
– a *road/town* map of...	– **une carte *routière/de la ville* de...** ewn kahrt *roo·teeyehr/duh lah veel* duh...
– stamps	– **des timbres** day tehN·bruh

> *i* You can find many English-language newspapers at newsstands in major cities, at airports and bus and train stations.

Photography

I'd like...camera.	**Je voudrais un appareil photo...** zhuh voo·dray zuhN nah·pah·rehy foh·toh...
– an automatic	– **automatique** oh·toh·mah·teek
– a digital	– **numérique** new·may·reek
– a disposable	– **jetable** zheh·tah·bluh
I'd like...	**Je voudrais...** zhuh voo·dray...
– a battery	– **une pile** ewn peel
– digital prints	– **des photos numériques** day foh·toh new·may·reek
– a memory card	– **une carte mémoire** ewn kahrt may·mwahr
Can I print digital photos here?	**Puis-je imprimer des photos numériques ici?** pwee·zhuh ehN·pree·may day foh·toh new·may·reek ee·see

Sports and Leisure

Essential

When's the game?	**Quand a lieu le match?** kawN tah leeyuh luh mahtch
Where's…?	**Où est…?** oo ay…
– the beach	– **la plage** lah plazh
– the park	– **le parc** luh pahrk
– the pool	– **la piscine** lah pee·seen
Is it safe to swim here?	**Est-ce que c'est sans danger de nager ici?** ehs kuh say sawN dawN·zhay duh nah·zhay ee·see
Can I rent [hire] clubs?	**Puis-je louer des clubs?** pwee·zhuh looway day kluhb
How much per hour?	**Combien ça coûte par heure?** kohN·beeyehN sah koot pahr uhr
How far is it to…?	**À quelle distance se trouve…?** ah kehl dees·tawNs suh troov…
Show me on the map, please.	**Montrez-moi sur la carte, s'il vous plaît.** mohN·tray·mwah sewr lah kahrt seel voo play

Spectator Sports

When's…(game/ race/tournament)?	**Quand a lieu (le match/la course/ le tournoi)…?** kawN tah leeyuh (luh mahtch/lah koors/luh toor·nwah)…
– the baseball	– **de baseball** duh bays·bohl
– the basketball	– **de basketball** duh bahs·keht·bohl
– the boxing	– **de boxe** duh bohks

– the cricket	– **de cricket** duh kree·keh
– the cycling	– **de cycliste** duh see·kleest
– the golf	– **de golf** duh gohlf
– the soccer [football]	– **de football** duh foot·bohl
– the tennis	– **de tennis** duh tay·nees
– the volleyball	– **de volley-ball** duh voh·lee·bohl
Who's playing?	**Qui joue?** kee zhoo
Where's the *racetrack/stadium*?	**Où est *la piste/le stade*?** oo ay *lah peest/luh stahd*
Where can I place a bet?	**Où puis-je parier?** oo pwee·zhuh pah·reeyay

▶For ticketing, see page 19.

Soccer is France's most popular sport. Water sports, such as canoeing, rafting, fishing and sailing, are also popular, not only on the coast, but along scenic lakes and rivers. France is home to the highest peaks in Europe across three mountain ranges: the Alps, the Pyrenees and the Massif Central. Skiing, snowboarding, snowshoeing, hiking and dog sledding are enjoyed there. Other popular sports include cycling, horseback riding, horse racing, golf, paragliding, parachuting and car racing. France is host to many world-renowned sporting events: **Tour de France** bicycle race, **Le Mans** car race and the International Tennis Championships, to name a few.

Casinos can be found in France, especially along the French Riviera. Sports betting is permitted only on horse races.

Participating

Where *is/are*...?	**Où *est/sont*...?** oo ay/sohN...
– the golf course	**– le terrain de golf** luh teh·rehN duh gohlf
– the gym	**– le gymnase** luh zheem·nahz
– the park	**– le parc** luh pahrk
– the tennis courts	**– les courts de tennis** lay koor duh tay·nees
How much per...?	**Combien ça coûte par...?** kohN·beeyehN sah koot pahr...
– day	**– jour** zhoor
– hour	**– heure** uhr
– game	**– partie** pahr·tee
– round	**– tour** toor
Can I rent [hire]...?	**Puis-je louer...?** pwee·zhuh looway...
– some clubs	**– des clubs** day kluhb
– some equipment	**– des équipements** day zay·keep·mawN
– a racket	**– une raquette** ewn rah·keht

At the Beach/Pool

Where's the *beach/pool*?	**Où est la *plage/piscine*?** oo ay lah plahzh/pee·seen
Is there a...?	**Y-a-t-il...?** yah·teel...
– kiddie pool	**– une pataugeoire** ewn pah·toh·zhwahr
– *indoor/outdoor* pool	**– une piscine *intérieure/extérieure*** ewn pee·seen ehN·tay·reeyuhr/ehks·tay·reeyuhr
– lifeguard	**– un secouriste** uhN suh·koo·reest
Is it safe...?	**Est-ce sans danger...?** ehs sawN dawN·zhay...
– to swim	**– de nager** duh nah·zhay
– to dive	**– de plonger** duh plohN·zhay
– for children	**– pour les enfants** poor lay zawN·fawN

I'd like to rent [hire]…	**Je voudrais louer…** zhuh voo·dray looway…
– a deck chair	– **une chaise** ewn shehz
– diving equipment	– **un équipement de plongée** uhN nay·keep·mawN duh plohN·zhay
– a jet ski	– **un jet ski** uhN zheht skee
– a motorboat	– **un bateau à moteur** uhN bah·toh ah moh·tuhr
– a rowboat	– **une barque** ewn bahrk
– snorkeling equipment	– **un équipement de plongée** uhN ay·keep·mawN duh plohN·zhay
– a surfboard	– **un surf** uhN suhrf
– a towel	– **une serviette** ewn sehr·veeyeht
– an umbrella	– **un parasol** uhN pah·rah·sohl
– water skis	– **des skis nautiques** day skee noh·teek
– a windsurfing board	– **une planche à voile** ewn plawNsh ah vwahl
For…hours.	**Pour…heures.** poor…uhr

France has many beaches; the country has long coasts on the English Channel, the Atlantic Ocean and the Mediterranean Sea. Some of France's most popular beach destinations include St. Tropez, Monte Carlo, Cannes, Marseilles, Nice and the island of Corsica in the Mediterranean. Most beaches are staffed with lifeguards during the summer months, but always check the flags for swimming conditions. A green flag indicates that swimming is allowed, an orange flag indicates swimming is allowed but hazardous, a red flag indicates swimming is not allowed and a yellow flag indicates swimming is inadvisable because of pollution.

Winter Sports

A lift pass for *a day/five days*, please.	**Un forfait** *d' un jour/de cinq jours***, s'il vous plaît.** uhN fohr·fay *duhN zhoor/duh sehNk zhoor* seel voo play
I'd like to rent [hire]…	**Je voudrais louer…** zhuh voo·dray looway…
– boots	**– des bottes** day boht
– a helmet	**– un casque** uhN kahsk
– poles	**– des bâtons** day bah·tohN
– skis	**– des skis** day skee
– a snowboard	**– un snowboard** uhN snoh·bohrd
– snowshoes	**– des raquettes** day rah·keht
These are too *big/small*.	**Ceux-ci♂/Celles-ci♀ sont trop** *grands♂/ grandes♀/petits♂/petites♀***.** suh·see♂/sehl·see♀ sohN troh *grawN♂/ grawNd♀/puh·tee♂/puh·teet♀*
Are there lessons?	**Y-a-t-il des leçons?** yah·teel day luh·sohN
I'm a beginner.	**Je suis débutant♂/débutante♀.** zhuh swee day·bew·tawN♂/day·bew·tawNt♀

I'm experienced.	**J'ai de l'expérience.** zhay duh lehk·spay·reeyawNs
A trail [piste] map, please.	**La carte des pistes, s'il vous plaît.** lah kahrt day peest seel voo play

You May See...

REMONTÉES	lifts
REMONTE-PENTES	drag lift
TÉLÉPHÉRIQUE	cable car
TÉLÉSIÈGE	chair lift
DÉBUTANT	novice
INTERMÉDIAIRE	intermediate
EXPERT	expert
PISTE FERMÉE	trail [piste] closed

In the Countryside

A map of..., please.	**Une carte..., s'il vous plaît.** ewn kahrt... seel voo play
– this region	**– de cette région** duh seht ray·zheeyohN
– the walking routes	**– des chemins de randonnées** day sheh·mehN duh rawN·doh·nay
– the bike routes	**– des pistes cyclables** day peest see·klah·bluh
– the trails	**– des sentiers** day sawN·teeyay
Is it...?	**Est-ce...?** ehs...
– easy	**– facile** fah·seel
– difficult	**– difficile** dee·fee·seel
– far	**– loin** lwehN
– steep	**– escarpé** ehs·kahr·pay

How far is it to…?	**À quelle distance se trouve…?** ah kehl dees·tawNs suh troov…
I'm lost.	**Je suis perdu♂/perdue♀.** zhuh swee pehr·dew
Where's…?	**Où est…?** oo ay…
– the bridge	**– le pont** luh pohN
– the cave	**– la grotte** lah groht
– the desert	**– le désert** luh day·zehr
– the farm	**– la ferme** lah fehrm
– the field	**– le champ** luh shawN
– the forest	**– la forêt** lah foh·reh
– the hill	**– la colline** lah koh·leen
– the lake	**– le lac** luh lahk
– the mountain	**– la montagne** lah mohN·tah·nyuh
– the nature preserve	**– le parc naturel** luh pahrk nah·tew·rehl
– the overlook [viewpoint]	**– le point d'observation** luh pwehN dohb·sehr·vah·seeyohN
– the park	**– le parc** luh pahrk
– the path	**– le chemin** luh shuh·mehN
– the peak	**– le sommet** luh soh·may
– the picnic area	**– l'aire de pique-nique** lehr duh peek·neek
– the pond	**– l'étang** lay·tawN
– the river	**– la rivière** lah ree·veeyehr
– the sea	**– la mer** lah mehr
– the (hot) spring	**– la source (d'eau chaude)** lah soors (doh shohd)
– the stream	**– le ruisseau** luh rwee·soh
– the valley	**– la vallée** lah vah·lay
– the vineyard	**– la vigne** lah vee·nyuh
– the waterfall	**– les cascades** lay kahs·kahd

Culture and Nightlife

Essential

What's there to do at night?	**Que peut-on faire le soir?** kuh puh·tohN fehr luh swahr
Do you have a program of events?	**Avez-vous un programme des festivités?** ah·vay·voo uhN proh·grahm day fehs·tee·vee·tay
What's playing tonight?	**Qui joue ce soir?** kee zhoo suh swahr
Where's...?	**Où est...?** oo ay...
– the downtown area	– **le centre ville** luh sawN·truh veel
– the bar	– **le bar** luh bahr
– the dance club	– **la discothèque** lah dees·koh·tehk

Entertainment

Can you recommend...?	**Pouvez-vous me conseiller...?** poo·vay·voo muh kohN·say·yay...
– a concert	– **un concert** uhN kohN·sehr
– a movie	– **un film** uhN feelm
– an opera	– **un opéra** uhN noh·pay·rah
– a play	– **une pièce de théâtre** ewn peeyehs duh tay·ah·truh
When does it *start/end*?	**Quand est-ce que ça *commence/finit*?** kawN tehs kuh sah *koh·mawNs/fee·nee*
What's the dress code?	**Quelle est la tenue exigée?** kehl ay lah tuh·new ehk·see·zhay

I like…	**J'aime…** zhehm…
– classical music	– **la musique classique** lah mew·zeek klah·seek
– folk music	– **la musique folklorique** lah mew·zeek fohl·kloh·reek
– jazz	– **le jazz** luh zhahz
– pop music	– **la pop musique** lah pohp mew·zeek
– rap	– **le rap** luh rahp

▶ For ticketing, see page 19.

 Tourist information offices can provide information on local entertainment. Newspapers will usually list upcoming events. In the larger cities, there are magazines and publications that list the bars, clubs and other venues and activities of interest. These magazines can usually be found in bookstores or newsstands. Your hotel concierge can also help you find entertainment options.

You May Hear...

Éteignez vos portables, s'il vous plaît.
ay·teh·nyay voh pohr·tah·bluh seel voo play

Turn off your cell
[mobile] phones,
please.

Nightlife

What's there to do
at night?

Que peut-on faire le soir? kuh puh·tohN fehr
luh swahr

Can you
recommend...?

Pouvez-vous me conseiller...? poo·vay·voo
muh kohN·say·yay...

– a bar

– un bar uhN bahr

– a cabaret

– un cabaret uhN kah·bah·ray

– a casino

– un casino uhN kah·zee·noh

– a dance club

– une discothèque ewn dees·koh·tehk

– a gay club

– un club gay uhN kluhb gay

– a jazz club

– un club de jazz uhN kluhb duh zhahz

– a club with
French music

– un club de musique française uhN kluhb
duh mew·zeek frawN·sehz

Is there live music?

Y-a-t-il des concerts? yah·teel day kohN·sehr

How do I get
there?

Comment est-ce que je m'y rends?
koh·mawN tehs kuh zhuh mee rawN

Is there a cover
charge?

Y-a-t-il un droit d'entrée? yah·teel uhN
drwah dawN·tray

Let's go dancing.

Allons danser. ah·lohN dawN·say

▼ Special Needs

Essential

I'm here on business.	**Je suis ici pour affaires.** zhuh swee zee•see poo rah•fehr
Here's my card.	**Voici ma carte.** vwah•see mah kahrt
Can I have your card?	**Puis-je avoir votre carte?** pwee•zhuh ah•vwahr voh•truh kahrt
I have a meeting with…	**J'ai une réunion avec…** zhay ewn ray•ew•neeyohN nah•vehk…
Where's…?	**Où est…?** oo ay…
– the business center	– **le centre d'affaires** luh sawN•truh dah•fehr
– the convention hall	– **le palais des congrès** luh pah•lay day kohN•greh
– the meeting room	– **la salle de réunion** lah sahl duh ray•ew•neeyohN

> ***i*** The customary greeting for business people is a firm handshake. Last names are used instead of first names when meeting someone; say, **Bonjour, monsieur/madame…**. It is polite to be on time for business meetings.

Business Communication

I'm here for…	**Je suis ici pour…** zhuh swee zee•see poor…
– a seminar	– **un séminaire** uhN say•mee•nehr
– a conference	– **une conférence** ewn kohN•fay•rawNs
– a meeting	– **une réunion** ewn ray•ew•neeyohN

My name is…	**Je m'appelle…** zhuh mah·pehl…
May I introduce my colleague…	**Puis-je vous présenter mon♂/ma♀ collègue…** pwee·zhuh voo pray·zawN·tay mohN♂/mah♀ koh·lehg…
I have *a meeting/an appointment* with…	**J'ai *une réunion/un rendez-vous* avec…** zhay *ewn ray·ew·neeyohN/uhN rawN·day·voo* ah·vehk…
I'm sorry I'm late.	**Je suis désolé♂/désolée♀, je suis en retard.** zhuh swee day·zoh·lay zhuh swee zawN ruh·tahr
I need an interpreter.	**J'ai besoin d'un interprète.** zhay buh·zwehN duhN nehN·tehr·preht
You can contact me at the…Hotel.	**Vous pouvez me joindre à l'hôtel…** voo poo·vay muh zhwehN·druh ah loh·tehl…
I'm here until…	**Je suis ici jusqu'à…** zhuh swee zee·see zhew·skah…
I need to…	**J'ai besoin…** zhay buh·zwehN…
– make a call	**– de téléphoner** duh tay·lay·foh·nay
– make a photocopy	**– de faire une photocopie** duh fehr ewn foh·toh·koh·pee
– send an e-mail	**– d'envoyer un mail** dawN·vwah·yay uhN mehl
– send a fax	**– d'envoyer un fax** dawN·vwah·yay uhN fahks
– send a package (for next-day delivery)	**– d'envoyer un colis (avec livraison le jour suivant)** dawN·vwah·yay uhN koh·lee (ah·vehk lee·vray·zohN luh zhoor swee·vawN)
It was a pleasure to meet you.	**J'ai été ravi♂/ravi♀ de faire votre connaissance.** zhay ay·tay rah·vee duh fehr voh·truh koh·neh·sawNs

▶For internet and communications, see page 49.

You May Hear…

Avez-vous un rendez-vous? ah·vay·voo
zuhN rawN·day·voo

Do you have an
appointment?

Avec qui? ah·vehk kee

With whom?

Il♂/Elle♀ est en réunion. eel♂/ehl♀ ay
tawN ray·ew·neeyohN

He/She is in
a meeting.

Un instant, s'il vous plaît. uhN nehN·stawN
seel voo play

One moment,
please.

Asseyez-vous. ah·seh·yay·voo

Have a seat.

Voulez-vous boire quelque chose?
voo·lay·voo bwahr kehl·kuh shohz

Would you like
something to drink?

Merci de votre visite. mehr·see duh
voh·truh vee·zeet

Thank you for
coming.

Essential

Is there a discount for kids?	**Y-a-t-il une remise pour les enfants?** yah-teel ewn ruh-meez poor lay zawN-fawN
Can you recommend a babysitter?	**Pouvez-vous me recommander une baby-sitter?** poo-vay-voo muh ruh-koh-mawN-day ewn bah-bee-see-tuhr
Do you have *a child's seat/highchair*?	**Avez-vous** *un siège enfant/une chaise haute*? ah-vay-voo *zuhN seeyehzh awN-fawN/ zewn shehz oht*
Where can I change the baby?	**Où puis-je changer le bébé?** oo pwee-zhuh shawN-zhay luh bay-bay

Fun with Kids

Can you recommend something for kids?	**Pouvez-vous me conseiller quelque chose pour les enfants?** poo-vay-voo muh kohN-say-yay kehl-kuh shohz poor lay zawN-fawN
Where's…?	**Où est…?** oo ay…
– the amusement park	– **le parc d'attractions** luh pahrk dah-trahk-seeyohN
– the arcade	– **la salle de jeux** lah sahl duh zhuh
– the kiddie [paddling] pool	– **la pataugeoire** lah pah-toh-zhwahr
– the park	– **le parc** luh pahrk
– the playground	– **l'aire de jeux** lehr duh zhuh
– the zoo	– **le zoo** luh zoh
Are kids allowed?	**Est-ce que les enfants sont autorisés?** ehs kuh lay zawN-fawN sohN toh-toh-ree-zay

Is it safe for kids?	**Est-ce que c'est sans danger pour les enfants?** ehs kuh say sawN dawN·zay poor lay zawN·fawN
Is it suitable for…year olds?	**Est-ce que cela convient aux enfants de…ans?** ehs kuh suh·lah kohN·veeyehN oh zawN·fawN duh…awN

▶For numbers, see page 173.

You May Hear…

Comme il♂/elle♀ est mignon♂/mignonne♀! kohm eel♂/ehl♀ ay mee·nyohN♂/mee·nyohn♀	How cute!
Comment s'appelle-t-il♂/elle♀? koh·mawN sah·pehl·teel♂/tehl♀	What's his/her name?
Quel âge a-t-il♂/a-t-elle♀? kehl ahzh ah·teel♂/ah·tehl♀	How old is he/she?

Basic Needs for Kids

Do you have...?	**Avez-vous...?** ah·vay·voo...
– a baby bottle	**– un biberon** uhN bee·buh·rohN
– baby food	**– des petits pots** day puh·tee poh
– baby wipes	**– des lingettes pour bébé** day lehN·zhet poor bay·bay
– a car seat	**– un siège bébé** uhN seeyehzh bay·bay
– a children's menu/portion	**– un menu/des portions pour enfants** uhN muh·new/day pohr·seeyohN poo rawN·fawN
– a child's seat/ highchair	**– un siège bébé/une chaise haute** uhN seeyehzh bay·bay/ewn shehz oht
– a crib/cot	**– un berceau/lit pliant** uhN behr·soh/ lee pleeyawN
– diapers [nappies]	**– des couches** day koosh
– formula [baby food]	**– du lait pour bébé** dew lay poor bay·bay
– a pacifier [soother]	**– une tétine** ewn tay·teen
– a playpen	**– un parc pour enfant** uhN pahrk poo rawN·fawN
– a stroller [pushchair]	**– une poussette** ewn poo·seht
Can I breastfeed the baby here?	**Puis-je allaiter le bébé ici?** pwee·zhuh ah·leh·tay luh bay·bay ee·see
Where can I breastfeed/change the baby?	**Où puis-je allaiter/changer le bébé?** oo pwee·zhuh ah·leh·tay/shawN·zhay luh bay·bay

▶For dining with kids, see page 65.

Babysitting

Can you recommend
a babysitter?

**Pouvez-vous me recommander une
baby-sitter?** poo·vay·voo muh
ruh·koh·mawN·day ewn bah·bee·see·tuhr

How much do
you/they charge?

Quel est *votre/leur* tarif? kehl ay *voh·truh/
luhr* tah·reef

I'll be back at…

Je reviens à… zhuh ruh·veeyehN ah…

▶ For time, see page 175.

If you need to contact
me, call…

**Si vous avez besoin de me contacter,
appelez…** see voo sah·vay buh·swehN duh
muh kohN·tahk·tay ah·play…

Health and Emergency

Can you recommend
a pediatrician?

**Pouvez-vous me recommander un
pédiatre?** poo·vay·voo muh ruh·koh·mawN·day
uhN pay·deeyah·truh

My child is
allergic to…

Mon enfant est allergique à… mohN
nawN·fawN ay ah·lehr·zheek ah…

My child is missing.

Mon enfant a disparu. mohN nawN·fawN ah
dees·pah·rew

Have you seen
a *boy/girl*?

Avez-vous vu *un garçon/une fille*?
ah·vay·voo vew *uhN gahr·sohN/ewn fee·yuh*

▶ For food items, see page 90.

▶ For health, see page 158.

▶ For police, see page 155.

For the Disabled

Essential

Is there...?	**Y-a-t-il...?** yah·teel...
– access for the disabled	– **un accès pour handicapés** uhN nahk·seh poor awN·dee·kah·pay
– a wheelchair ramp	– **un accès pour chaises roulantes** uhN nahk·say poor shehz roo·lawNt
– a handicapped-[disabled-] accessible toilet	– **des toilettes accessibles aux handicapés** day twah·leht ahk·seh·see·bluh oh awN·dee·kah·pay
I need...	**J'ai besoin...** zhay buh·zwehN...
– assistance	– **d'aide** dehd
– an elevator [a lift]	– **d'un ascenseur** duhN nah·sawN·suhr
– a ground-floor room	– **d'une chambre au rez-de-chaussée** dewn shawN·bruh oh ray·duh·shoh·say

Getting Help

I'm...	**Je suis...** zhuh swee...
– disabled	– **handicapé♂/handicapée♀** awN·dee·kah·pay
– visually impaired	– **malvoyant♂/malvoyante♀** mahl·vwah·yawN ♂/mahl·vwah·yawNt ♀
– deaf	– **sourd♂/sourde♀** soor♂/soord♀
– hearing impaired	– **malentendant♂/malentendante♀** mah·lawN·tawN·dawN♂/mah·lawN·tawN·dahNt♀
– unable to *walk far/use the stairs*	– **incapable *de marcher longtemps/d'utiliser les escaliers*** ehN·kah·pah·bluh *duh mahr·shay lohN·tawN/dew·tee·lee·zay lay zehs·kah·leeyay*

Please speak louder.	**S'il vous plaît, parlez plus fort.** seel voo play pahr·lay plew fohr
Can I bring my wheelchair?	**Puis-je apporter ma chaise roulante?** pwee·zhuh ah·pohr·tay mah shehz roo·lawNt
Are guide dogs permitted?	**Est-ce que les chiens de guide sont autorisés?** ehs kuh lay sheeyehN duh geed sohN toh·toh·ree·zay
Can you help me?	**Pouvez-vous m'aider?** poo·vay·voo mehy·day
Please *open/hold* the door.	**S'il vous plaît, *ouvrez/tenez* la porte.** seel voo play *oo·vray/tuh·nay* lah pohrt

▼ Resources

Emergencies

Essential

Help!	**Au secours!** oh suh·koor
Go away!	**Allez-vous en!** ah·lay·voo zawN
Stop, thief!	**Arrêtez, au voleur!** ah·reh·tay oh voh·luhr
Get a doctor!	**Allez chercher un docteur!** ah·lay shehr·shay uhN dohk·tuhr
Fire!	**Au feu!** oh fuh
I'm lost.	**Je suis perdu♂/perdue♀.** zhuh swee pehr·dew
Can you help me?	**Pouvez-vous m'aider?** poo·vay·voo may·day

Police

Essential

Call the police!	**Appelez la police!** ah·puh·lay lah poh·lees
Where's the police station?	**Où est le commissariat de police?** oo ay luh koh·mee·sah·reeyah duh poh·lees
There was an *accident/attack*.	**Il y a eu *un accident/une attaque*.** eel·yah ew *uhN nahk·see·dawN/ewn ah·tahk*
My child is missing.	**Mon enfant a disparu.** mohN nawN·fawN ah dees·pah·rew
I need *an interpreter/to make a phone call*.	**J'ai besoin *d'un interprète/de téléphoner*.** zhay buh·zwehN *duhN nehN·tehr·preht/ duh tay·lay·foh·nay*
I'm innocent.	**Je suis innocent♂/innocente♀.** zhuh swee zee·noh·sawN♂/zee·noh·sawNt♀

You May Hear...

Remplissez ce formulaire. rawN·plee·say suh fohr·mew·lehr — Fill out this form.

Vos papiers d'identité, s'il vous plaît. voh pah·peeyay dee·dawN·tee·tay seel voo play — Your ID, please.

Quand/Où **cela s'est-il produit?** *kawN/oo* suh·lah say·teel proh·dwee — *When/Where* did it happen?

À quoi ressemble-t-il♂/ ressemble-t-elle♀? ah kwah ruh·sawN·bluh·teel♂/ruh·sawN·bluh·tehl♀ — What does he/she look like?

i Contact your consulate, ask the concierge at your hotel or ask the tourist information office for telephone numbers of the local ambulance, emergency services and police.

Lost Property and Theft

I'd like to report...	**Je voudrais signaler...** zhuh voo·dray see·nyah·lay...
– a mugging	– **une attaque** ewn ah·tahk
– a rape	– **un viol** uhN veeyohl
– a theft	– **un vol** uhN vohl
I was mugged.	**J'ai été attaqué♂/attaquée♀.** zhay ay·tay ah·tah·kay
I was robbed.	**J'ai été dévalisé♂/dévalisée♀.** zhay ay·tay day·vah·lee·zay
I lost...	**J'ai perdu...** zhay pehr·dew...
...was stolen.	**...a été volé♂/volée♀.** ...ah ay·tay voh·lay
– My backpack	– **Mon sac-à-dos** mohN sahk·ah·doh
– My bicycle	– **Mon vélo** mohN vay·loh
– My camera	– **Mon appareil photo** mohN nah·pah·rehy foh·toh
– My (rental [hire]) car	– **Ma voiture (de location)** mah vwah·tuhr (duh loh·kah·seeyohN)
– My computer	– **Mon ordinateur** mohN nohr·dee·nah·tuhr
– My credit card	– **Ma carte de crédit** mah kahrt duh kray·dee
– My jewelry	– **Mes bijoux** may bee·zhoo
– My money	– **Mon argent** mohN nahr·zhawN
– My passport	– **Mon passeport** mohN pahs·pohr
– My purse [handbag]	– **Mon sac** mohN sahk
– My traveler's checks [cheques]	– **Mes chèques de voyage** may shehk duh vwah·yahzh
– My wallet	– **Mon porte-feuille** mohN pohrt·fuhy
I need a police report.	**J'ai besoin d'un constat de police.** zhay buh·zwehN duhN kohN·stah duh poh·lees

Health

I'm sick [ill].	**Je suis malade.** zhuh swee mah·lahd
I need an English-speaking doctor.	**J'ai besoin d'un docteur qui parle anglais.** zhay buh·zwehN duhN dohk·tuhr kee pahrl awN·glay
It hurts here.	**Ça fait mal ici.** sah fay mahl ee·see

Finding a Doctor

Can you recommend a *doctor/dentist*?	**Pouvez-vous me recommander un *docteur/dentiste*?** poo·vay·voo muh ruh·koh·mawN·day uhN *dohk·tuhr/dawN·teest*
Can the doctor come here?	**Est-ce que le docteur peut venir ici?** ehs kuh luh dohk·tuhr puh veh·neer ee·see
I need an English-speaking doctor.	**J'ai besoin d'un docteur qui parle anglais.** zhay buh·zwehN duhN dohk·tuhr kee pahrl awN·glay
What are the office hours?	**Quelles sont les heures d'ouverture?** kehl sohN lay zuhr doo·vehr·tewr
I'd like an appointment for...	**Je voudrais un rendez-vous pour...** zhuh voo·dray uhN rawN·day·voo poor...
– today	– **aujourd'hui** oh·zhoor·dwee
– tomorrow	– **demain** duh·mehN
– as soon as possible	– **le plus vite possible** luh plew veet poh·see·bluh
It's urgent.	**C'est urgent.** say tewr·zhawN

Symptoms

I'm bleeding.	**Je saigne.** zhuh sehnyuh
I'm constipated.	**Je suis constipé**♂**/constipée**♀. zhuh swee kohN·stee·pay
I'm dizzy.	**J'ai des vertiges.** zhay day vehr·teezh
I'm nauseous.	**J'ai des nausées.** zhay day noh·zay
I'm vomiting.	**Je vomis.** zhuh voh·mee
It hurts here.	**J'ai mal ici.** zhay mahl ee·see
I have…	**J'ai…** zhay…
– an allergic reaction	– **une réaction allergique** ewn reh·ahk·seeyohN ah·lehr·zheek
– chest pain	– **une douleur à la poitrine** ewn doo·luhr ah lah pwah·treen
– cramps	– **des crampes** day krawNp
– diarrhea	– **la diarrhée** lah deeyah·ray
– an earache	– **mal aux oreilles** mahl oh zoh·rehy
– a fever	– **de la fièvre** duh lah feeyeh·vruh
– pain	– **mal** mahl
– a rash	– **une irritation cutanée** ewn ee·ree·tah·seeyohN kew·tah·nay
– a sprain	– **une entorse** ewn awN·tohrs
– some swelling	– **une grosseur** ewn groh·suhr
– a sore throat	– **un mal de gorge** uhN mahl duh gohrzh
– a stomachache	– **mal au ventre** mahl oh vawN·truh
I've been sick [ill] for…days.	**Je suis malade depuis…jours.** zhuh swee mah·lahd duh·pwee…zhoor

▶ For numbers, see page 173.

Health Conditions

I'm...	**Je suis...** zhuh swee...
– anemic	– **anémique** ah·nay·meek
– asthmatic	– **asthmatique** ahs·mah·teek
– diabetic	– **diabétique** deeyah·bay·teek
– I'm allergic to *antibiotics/ penicillin.*	– **Je suis allergique** *aux antibiotiques/à la pénicilline.* zhuh swee zah·lehr·zheek oh zawN·tee·beeyoh·teek/ah lah pay·nee·see·leen

▶ For food items, see page 90.

I have...	**J'ai...** zhay...
– arthritis	– **de l'arthrite** duh lahr·treet
– a heart condition	– **un problème cardiaque** uhN proh·blehm kahr·deeyahk
– *high/low* blood pressure	– **une tension** *élevée/basse* ewn tawN·seeyohN *ay·luh·vay/bahs*
I'm on...	**Je prends...** zhuh prawN...

You May Hear...

Qu'est-ce qui ne va pas? kehs kee nuh vah pah	What's wrong?
Où est-ce que ça fait mal? oo ehs kuh sah fay mahl	Where does it hurt?
Est-ce que ça fait mal ici? ehs kuh sah fay mahl ee·see	Does it hurt here?
Prenez-vous des médicaments? prueh·nay·voo day may·dee·kah·mawN	Are you on medication?
Êtes-vous allergique à quelque chose? eht·voo zah·lehr·zheek ah kehl·kuh shohz	Are you allergic to anything?

Ouvrez la bouche. oo·vray lah boosh · Open your mouth.

Respirez profondément. rehs·pee·ray proh·fohN·day·mawN · Breathe deeply.

Toussez, s'il vous plaît. too·say seel voo play · Cough, please.

Allez à l'hôpital. ah·lay ah loh·pee·tahl · Go to the hospital.

Treatment

Do I need a *prescription/ medicine*? | **Ai-je besoin *d'une ordonnance/de médicaments*?** ay·zhuh buh·zwehN *dewn ohr·doh·nawNs/duh meh·dee·kah·mawN*

Can you prescribe a generic drug [unbranded medication]? | **Pouvez-vous me prescrire un médicament générique?** poo·vay·voo muh prehs·kreer uhN may·dee·kah·mawN zhay·nay·reek

Where can I get it? | **Où puis-je l'obtenir?** oo pwee·zhuh lohb·tuh·neer

▶ For dosage instructions, see page 164.

Hospital

Notify my family, please. | **Informez ma famille, s'il vous plaît.** ehN·fohr·may mah fah·meeyuh seel voo play

I'm in pain. | **J'ai mal.** zhay mahl

I need a *doctor/nurse*. | **J'ai besoin *d'un docteur/d'une infirmière*.** zhay buh·zwehN *duhN dohk·tuhr/dewn ehN·feer·meeyehr*

When are visiting hours? | **Quand sont les heures de visite?** kawN sohN lay zuhr duh vee·zeet

I'm visiting… | **Je viens voir…** zhuh veeyehN vwahr…

Dentist

I have...	**J'ai...** zhay...
– a broken tooth	**– une dent cassée** ewn dawN kah·say
– a lost filling	**– perdu ♂/perdue ♀ un plombage** pehr·dew uhN plohN·bahzh
– a toothache	**– mal aux dents** mahl oh dawN
Can you fix this denture?	**Pouvez-vous réparer ce dentier?** poo·vay·voo ray·pah·ray suh dawN·teeyay

Gynecologist

I have *cramps/ a vaginal infection*.	**J'ai *des crampes/une infection vaginale*.** zhay day krawNp/ewn ehN·fehk·seeyohN vah·zhee·nahl
I missed my period.	**Je n'ai pas eu mes règles.** zhuh nay pah ew may reh·gluh
I'm on the Pill.	**Je prends la pillule.** zhuh prawN lah pee·lewl
I'm (...months) pregnant.	**Je suis enceinte (de...mois).** zhuh swee zawN·sehNt (duh...mwah)
I'm not pregnant.	**Je ne suis pas enceinte.** zhuh nuh swee pah zawN·sehNt
My last period was...	**Mes dernières règles étaient...** may dehr·neeyehr reh·gluh ay·tay...

▶ For numbers, see page 173.

Optician

I lost...	**J'ai perdu...** zhay pehr·dew...
– a contact lens	**– une lentille de contact** ewn lawN·tee·yuh duh kohN·tahk
– my glasses	**– mes lunettes** may lew·neht
– a lens	**– une lentille** ewn lawN·tee·yuh

Payment and Insurance

How much?	**Combien ça coûte?** kohN·beeyehN sah koot
Can I pay by credit card?	**Puis-je payer par carte?** pwee·zhuh pay·yay pahr kahrt
I have insurance.	**J'ai une assurance.** zhay ewn ah·sew·rawNs
I need a receipt for my insurance.	**J'ai besoin d'un reçu pour ma compagnie d'assurance.** zhay buh·zwehN duhN ruh·sew poor mah kohN·pah·nee dah·sew·rawNs

Pharmacy [Chemist]

Essential

Where's the pharmacy [chemist]?	**Où est la pharmacie?** oo ay lah fahr·mah·see
What time does it *open/close*?	**À quelle heure *ouvre-t-elle/ferme-t-elle*?** ah kehl uhr *oo·vruh·tehl/fehrm·tehl*
What would you recommend for…?	**Que me conseillez-vous pour…?** kuh muh kohN·say·yay·voo poor…
How much do I take?	**Combien dois-je en prendre?** kohN·beeyehN dwah·zhuh awN prawN·druh
I'm allergic to…	**Je suis allergique à…** zhuh swee zah·lehr·zheek ah…

Pharmacies can be identified by the green cross-shaped neon light on display. Pharmacies are usually open from 9 a.m. to 6 p.m. without closing for lunch. Some pharmacies are open from 8 a.m. to 2 a.m. or even 24 hours, especially in the larger cities; a list of 24-hour pharmacies can be found on the door of every pharmacy. Some doctors still make house calls; ask your concierge for more information.

Dosage Instructions

How much do I take?	**Combien dois-je en prendre?** kohN·beeyehN dwah·zhuh awN prawN·druh
How often?	**Combien de fois?** kohN·beeyehN duh fwah
Is it safe for children?	**Est-ce sans danger pour les enfants?** ehs sawN dawN·zay poor lay zawN·fawN
I'm taking…	**Je prends…** zhuh prawN…
Are there side effects?	**Y-a-t-il des effets secondaires?** yah·teel day zeh·feh suh·kohN·dehr

You May See...

UNE/TROIS FOIS PAR JOUR	*once/three* times a day
UN CACHET	tablet
UNE GOUTTE	drop
UNE CUILLÈRE	teaspoon
...LES REPAS	...meals
– APRÈS	– after
– AVANT	– before
– PENDANT	– with
À JEUN	on an empty stomach
À AVALER	swallow whole
RISQUE DE SOMNOLENCE	may cause drowsiness
NE PAS AVALER	do not ingest

Health Problems

I need something for...	**J'ai besoin de quelque chose pour soigner...** zhay buh·zwehN duh kehl·kuh shohz poor swah·nyay...
– a cold	– **un rhume** uhN rewm
– a cough	– **une toux** ewn too
– diarrhea	– **une diarrhée** ewn deeyah·ray
– insect bites	– **des piqures d'insectes** day pee·kewr dehN·sehkt
– motion [travel] sickness	– **le mal des transports** luh mahl day trawNs·pohr
– a sore throat	– **un mal à la gorge** uhN mahl ah lah gohrzh
– sunburn	– **un coup de soleil** uhN koo duh soh·lehy
– an upset stomach	– **un mal au ventre** uhN mahl oh vawN·truh

Basic Needs

I'd like...   **Je voudrais...** zhuh voo·dray...

– acetaminophen [paracetamol]
– **du paracétamol** dew pah·rah·say·tah·mohl

– antiseptic cream
– **une crème antiseptique** ewn krehm awN·tee·sehp·teek

– aspirin
– **une aspirine** ewn ahs·pee·reen

– bandages
– **des pansements** day pawNs·mawN

– a comb
– **un peigne** uhN peh·nyuh

– condoms
– **des préservatifs** day pray·sehr·vah·teef

– contact lens solution
– **de la solution pour lentilles de contact** duh lah soh·lew·seeyohN poor lawN·tee·yuh duh kohN·tahk

– deodorant
– **du déodorant** dew day·oh·doh·rawN

– a hairbrush
– **une brosse à cheveux** ewn brohs ah shuh·vuh

– hairspray
– **de la laque** duh lah lahk

– ibuprofen
– **de l'ibuprofène** duh lee·bew·proh·fehn

– insect repellent
– **de la lotion anti-insectes** duh lah loh·seeyohN awN·tee·ehN·sehkt

– lotion
– **une lotion** ewn loh·seeyohN

– a nail file
– **une lime à ongle** ewn leem ah ohN·gluh

– a (disposable) razor
– **un rasoir (jetable)** uhN rah·zwahr (zhuh·tah·bluh)

– razor blades
– **des lames de rasoir** day lahm duh rah·zwahr

– sanitary napkins [pads]
– **des serviettes hygiéniques** day sehr·veeyeht ee·zheeyay·neek

– shampoo/ conditioner
– **du shampooing/de l'après shampooing** dew shawN·poo·weeng/duh lah·preh shawN·poo·weeng

– soap
– **du savon** dew sah·vohN

- sunscreen — **de la crème solaire** duh lah krehm soh·lehr
- tampons — **des tampons** day tawN·pohN
- tissues — **des Kleenex®** day klee·nehks
- toilet paper — **du papier toilette** dew pah·peeyay twah·leht
- toothpaste — **du dentifrice** dew dehN·tee·frees

▶ For baby products, see page 150.

Reference

Grammar

Regular Verbs and Their Tenses

Regular French verbs follow a set pattern for conjugation. Remove the **-er**, **-ir** or **-re** ending and replace it with the correct ending for the tense and gender. See the tables below for examples of regular **-er**, **-ir** and **-re** verbs and the appropriate endings (in bold).

French uses subject pronouns (I, you, he, etc.) in much the same ways as English does. The first-person singular subject pronoun (I) is **je**. **Je** is abbreviated to **j'** if the following word begins with a vowel.

The following abbreviations are used in this section: sing. = singular; pl. = plural; inf. = informal; for. = formal.

PARLER (to speak)		Present	Past	Future
I	**je/j'**	parl**e**	ai parlé	parler**ai**
you (sing.)	**tu**	parl**es**	as parlé	parler**as**
he/she	**il**♂ **/elle**♀	parl**e**	a parlé	parler**a**
we	**nous**	parl**ons**	avons parlé	parler**ons**
you (pl.)	**vous**	parl**ez**	avez parlé	parler**ez**
they	**ils**♂ **/elles**♀	parl**ent**	ont parlé	parler**ont**

CHOISIR (to choose)		Present	Past	Future
I	je/j'	choisis	ai choisi	choisirai
you (sing.)	tu	choisis	as choisi	choisiras
he/she	il ♂/elle ♀	choisit	a choisi	choisira
we	nous	choisissons	avons choisi	choisirons
you (pl.)	vous	choisissez	avez choisi	choisirez
they	ils ♂/elles ♀	choisissent	ont choisi	choisiront

ATTENDRE (to wait for)		Present	Past	Future
I	je/j'	attends	ai attendu	attendrai
you (sing.)	tu	attends	as attendu	attendras
he/she	il ♂/elle ♀	attend	a attendu	attendra
we	nous	attendons	avons attendu	attendrons
you (pl.)	vous	attendez	avez attendu	attendrez
they	ils ♂/elles ♀	attendent	ont attendu	attendrent

Irregular Verbs

There are many irregular verbs that do not follow the standard conjugation rules and must be memorized. Two common irregular verbs are **avoir** (to have) and **être** (to be). **Avoir** and **être** are used as auxiliary verbs in the past tense. Most verbs use **avoir**, but several common, important verbs use **être**. In general, verbs of coming and going use **être** in the past tense, e.g., **aller** (to go), **venir** (to come), **sortir** (to go out), **partir** (to leave) and **arriver** (to arrive).

AVOIR (to have)	
I have	j'ai
you (sing.) have	tu as
he/she has	il ♂/elle ♀ a
we have	nous avons
you (pl.) have	vous avez
they have	ils ♂/elles ♀ ont

ÊTRE (to be)

I am	**je suis**
you (sing.) are	**tu es**
he/she is	**il ♂/elle ♀ est**
we are	**nous sommes**
you (pl.) are	**vous êtes**
they are	**ils ♂/elles ♀ sont**

Word Order

French sentences are constructed as in English: subject, verb, object.

Example: **Nous achetons un livre.** We're buying a book.

Questions can be formed in four different ways. The easiest is to just raise your voice at the end of a sentence:

Vous parlez anglais? You speak English?

You can also add **n'est-ce pas** (isn't that so/right) at the end of a phrase:

Vous parlez anglais, n'est-ce pas? You speak English, right?

You can put **est-ce que** in front of a phrase:

Est-ce que vous parlez anglais? Do you speak English?

You can also put the verb before the subject:

Parlez-vous anglais? Do you speak English?
(literally: Speak you English?)

Negations

Negative sentences are generally formed by adding **ne** before the verb and **pas** after it. When spoken, the **ne** is often dropped.

Example: **Nous fumons.** We smoke.

Nous ne fumons pas. We do not smoke.

Imperatives

Most imperatives are formed by using the stem of the verb with the appropriate ending.

you (sing.)	**tu**	**Parle!**	Speak!	**Attends!**	Wait!
we	**nous**	**Parlons!**	Let's speak!	**Attendons!**	Let's wait!
you (pl.)	**vous**	**Parlez!**	Speak!	**Attendez!**	Wait!

Nouns and Articles

In French, nouns are either masculine or feminine. Generally, nouns ending in **-e, -té** and **-tion** are feminine.

The singular definite articles (the) are **le**, for masculine nouns, and **la**, for feminine nouns. **Les** is the plural definite article for both masculine and feminine nouns.

Gender	Singular		Plural	
masculine	**le train**	the train	**les trains**	the trains
feminine	**la table**	the table	**les tables**	the tables

The singular indefinite articles (a/an) are **un**, for masculine nouns, and **une**, for feminine nouns. **Des** is the plural indefinite article for both masculine and feminine nouns.

Gender	Singular		Plural	
masculine	**un train**	a train	**des trains**	trains
feminine	**une table**	a table	**des tables**	tables

Adjectives

Adjectives describe nouns and must agree with the noun in gender and number. To form the feminine of many common adjectives, add **-e** to the masculine; if the word already ends in **-e** there is no change. To form the plural adjective, add **-s** to the end; if the word already ends in **-s** there is no change.

Examples:

un livre intéressant an interesting book

des livres intéresssants interesting books

une fille intéressante an interesting girl

des filles intéressantes interesting girls

Comparatives and Superlatives

Comparatives are formed by adding **plus** (more) or **moins** (less) before the adjective. Superlatives are formed by adding **le♂/la♀ plus** (most) or **le♂/la♀ moins** (least) before the adjective.

Example:

le vin sec the dry wine

le vin plus sec the drier wine

le vin le plus sec the driest wine

la bague chère the expensive ring

la bague moins chère the less expensive ring

la bague la moins chère the least expensive ring

Possessive Adjectives

Possessive adjectives come before the noun and must agree in gender and number with the noun/object, not the person possessing the object.

	Masculine	Feminine	Plural
my	**mon**	ma	mes
your (sing.)	**ton**	ta	tes
his/her	**son**	sa	ses
our	**notre**	notre	nos
your (pl.)	**votre**	votre	vos
their	**leur**	leur	leurs

Example: **Où sont *nos* passeports? Cherchons dans *mon* sac et dans *ta* valise.** Where are *our* passports? Let's look in *my* purse and in *your* suitcase.

Adverbs and Adverbial Expressions

Adverbs describe verbs. They are often formed by adding **-ment** to the feminine form of the adjective.

Examples:

Nous prenons le train lent. We are taking the slow train.

Jean conduit lentement. Jean drives slowly.

Il prends la route rapide. He is taking the fast route.

Frédérique conduit rapidement. Frédérique drives fast.

Prepositions

Prepositions are paired with nouns or verbs to create descriptive phrases. In French, several important prepositions form contractions when they appear in front of certain other words.

Some/Any

To express how much of something (to eat, to buy, etc.), French uses a construction called the partitive. The partitive is similar to some or any in English, and it is formed by combining **de** with the definite article (**le**, **la** or **les**). Even if some or any is not explicit in English, the partitive is always used in French.

Examples:

de + la ♀ (sing.) = de la	**Je voudrais de la soupe.** I'd like some soup.
de + le ♂ (sing.) = du	**Avez-vous commandé du fromage?** Did you order any cheese?
de + l' (before a vowel) = de l'	**Nous n'avons assez de l'eau.** We don't have enough water.
de + les (pl.) = des	**Il achete des chaussures.** He is buying shoes.

At/To

French expressions that use the word **à** are formed somewhat like the phrases using **de**.

Examples:

à + la ♀ (sing.) = **à la**	**Je vais à la plage.** I am going to the beach.
à + le ♂ (sing.) = **au**	**Nous restons au musée.** We're staying at the museum.
à + l' (before a vowel) = **à l'**	**Elles sont à l'église.** They are at the church.
à + les (pl.) = **aux**	**Ils partons aux gares.** They are leaving for the train station.

Numbers ————————————————

Essential	
0	**zéro** zay·roh
1	**un** uhN
2	**deux** duh
3	**trois** trwah
4	**quatre** kah·truh
5	**cinq** sehNk
6	**six** sees
7	**sept** seht
8	**huit** weet
9	**neuf** nuhf
10	**dix** dees
11	**onze** ohNz
12	**douze** dooz

13	**treize** trehz	
14	**quatorze** kah·tohrz	
15	**quinze** kehNz	
16	**seize** sehz	
17	**dix-sept** dee·seht	
18	**dix-huit** deez·weet	
19	**dix-neuf** deez·nuhf	
20	**vingt** vehN	
21	**vingt-et-un** vehN·tay·uhN	
22	**vingt-deux** vehN·duh	
30	**trente** trawNt	
31	**trente-et-un** trawN·tay·uhN	
40	**quarante** kah·rawNt	
50	**cinquante** sehN·kawNt	
60	**soixante** swah·zawNt	
70	**soixante-dix** swah·zawNt·dees	
80	**quatre-vingt** kah·truh·vehN	
90	**quatre-vingt-dix** kah·truh·vehN·dees	
100	**cent** sawN	
101	**cent-un** sawN·uhN	
200	**deux-cent** duh·sawN	
500	**cinq-cent** sehNk·sawN	
1,000	**mille** meel	
10,000	**dix mille** dee meel	
1,000,000	**un million** uhN meel·yohN	

Ordinal Numbers

first	**premier** ♂ /**première** ♀	pruh·meeyay ♂ / pruh·meeyehr ♀
second	**deuxième**	duh·zeeyehm
third	**troisième**	trwah·zeeyehm
fourth	**quatrième**	kah·treeyehm
fifth	**cinquième**	sehN·keeyehm
once	**une fois**	ewn fwah
twice	**deux fois**	duh fwah
three times	**trois fois**	trwah fwah

Time

Essential

What time is it?	**Quelle heure est-il?** kehl uhr ay·teel
It's noon [midday].	**Il est midi.** ee lay mee·dee
At midnight.	**À minuit.** ah mee·nwee
From one o'clock to two o'clock.	**D'une heure à deux heures.** dewn nuhr ah duh zuhr
Five after [past] three.	**Trois heures cinq.** trwah zuhr sehNk
A quarter to ten.	**Dix heures moins le quart.** dee zuhr mwehN luh kahr
5:30 *a.m./p.m.*	**Cinq heures et demi *du matin/de l'après-midi.*** sehN kuhr eh duh·mee *dew mah·tehN/duh lah·preh·mee·dee*

i

In France, the 24-hour clock is used for time, especially in schedules. The morning hours from 1:00 a.m. to noon are the same as in English. After that, just add 12 to the time: 1:00 p.m. would be 13:00, 5:00 p.m. would be 17:00 and so on.

In ordinary conversation, time is generally expressed using the 12-hour clock, with the addition of **du matin** (morning/a.m.), **de l'après-midi** (afternoon) or **du soir** (evening/p.m.).

Days

Essential

Monday	**lundi** luhN·dee
Tuesday	**mardi** mahr·dee
Wednesday	**mercredi** mehr·kruh·dee
Thursday	**jeudi** zhuh·dee
Friday	**vendredi** vawN·druh·dee
Saturday	**samedi** sahm·dee
Sunday	**dimanche** dee·mawNsh

Unlike those in the U.S., calendars in France are organized Monday to Sunday.

Dates

yesterday	**hier** eeyehr
today	**aujourd'hui** oh·zhoor·dwee
tomorrow	**demain** duh·mehN
day	**le jour** luh zhoor
week	**la semaine** lah suh·mehN
month	**le mois** luh mwah
year	**l'année/l'an** lah·nay/lawN

 France follows a day-month-year format instead of the month-day-year format favored in the U.S.

Examples: **le vingt-cinq juillet deux mille huit** = July 25, 2008; **25/07/08** = 7/25/2008

Months

January	**janvier** zhawN·veeyay
February	**février** fay·vreeyay
March	**mars** mahrs
April	**avril** ah·vreel
May	**mai** may
June	**juin** zhwehN
July	**juillet** zhwee·yay
August	**août** oot
September	**septembre** sehp·tawN·bruh
October	**octobre** ohk·toh·bruh

| November | **novembre** noh·vawN·bruh |
| December | **décembre** day·sawN·bruh |

Seasons

spring	**le printemps** luh prehN·tawN
summer	**l'été** lay·tay
fall [autumn]	**l'automne** loh·tohNn
winter	**l'hiver** lee·vehr

Holidays

Official Public Holidays

January 1: New Year's Day, **Le Nouvel An**

May 1: Labor Day, **La Fête du Travail**

May 8: Victory Day, **La Fête de la Libération**

July 14: Bastille Day, **La Fête Nationale**

August 15: Assumption Day, **L'Assomption**

November 1: All Saints Day, **La Toussaint**

November 11: Armistice Day, **L'Armistice**

December 25: Christmas, **Le Noël**

Moveable Feasts/Holidays

Good Friday, **Le Vendredi Saint**

Easter, **Le Pâques**

Easter Monday, **Le Lundi de Pâques**

Ascension, **L'Ascension**

Pentecost, **La Pentecôte**

i

The most important public holiday is **La Fête Nationale** (Bastille Day) on July 14. This holiday symbolizes the victory of the revolutionaries over the monarchy in 1789, creating the basis for the French Republic. **La Marseillaise**, the French national anthem, was created during the French Revolution, along with France's motto: **Liberté, Égalité, Fraternité** (Liberty, Equality, Brotherhood). The evening before July 14, people go to cafes and improvised dance areas; it is a festive atmosphere with dancing and celebration. There are firework displays throughout France that evening and on the 14th. The French president and members of the government, as well as other dignitaries, attend the **défilé**, a large military parade, on the Champs Élysées on Bastille Day.

Conversion Tables

When you know	Multiply by	To find
ounces	28.3	grams
pounds	0.45	kilograms
inches	2.54	centimeters
feet	0.3	meters
miles	1.61	kilometers
square inches	6.45	sq. centimeters
square feet	0.09	sq. meters
square miles	2.59	sq. kilometers
pints (U.S./Brit)	0.47/0.56	liters
gallons (U.S./Brit)	3.8/4.5	liters
Fahrenheit	5/9, after −32	Centigrade
Centigrade	9/5, then +32	Fahrenheit

Mileage

1 km	0.62 miles
5 km	3.1 miles
10 km	6.2 miles
50 km	31 miles
100 km	62 miles

Measurement

1 gram	**un gramme** uhN grahm	= 1000 milligrams	= 0.035 oz.
1 pound (lb)	**une livre** ewn lee·vruh	= 500 grams	= 1.1 lb
1 kilogram (kg)	**un kilo(gramme)** uhN kee·loh (grahm)	= 1000 grams	= 2.2 lb
1 liter (l)	**un litre** uhN lee·truh	= 1000 milliliters	= 1.06 U.S./0.88 Brit. Quarts
1 centimeter (cm)	**un centimètre** uhN sawN·tee·meh·truh	= 10 millimeters	= 0.4 inch
1 meter (m)	**un mètre** uhN meh·truh	= 100 centimeters	= 39.37 inches/ 3.28 ft.
1 kilometer (km)	**un kilomètre** uhN kee·loh·meh·truh	= 1000 meters	= 0.62 mile

Temperature

-40°C – -40°F	-1°C – 30°F	20°C – 68°F
-30°C – -22°F	0°C – 32°F	25°C – 77°F
-20°C – -4°F	5°C – 41°F	30°C – 86°F
-10°C – 14°F	10°C – 50°F	35°C – 95°F
-5°C – 23°F	15°C – 59°F	

Oven Temperature

100°C – 212°F	177°C – 350°F
121°C – 250°F	204°C – 400°F
149°C – 300°F	260°C – 500°F

Useful Websites

www.tsa.gov
U.S. Transportation Security Administration (TSA)

www.caa.co.uk
U.K. Civil Aviation Authority (CAA)

www.sncf.fr
France's national train system information

www.franceguide.com
France's tourist office

en.wikipedia.org/wiki/
international_clothing-sizes
Listing of International clothing sizes

English–French Dictionary

A

abbey l'abbaye
accept v accepter
access v accéder; n accés
accident l'accident
accommodation le logement
account le compte
acetaminophen le paracétamol
acupuncture l'acupuncture
adapter l'adaptateur
address l'adresse
admission l'entrée
after après; **~noon** l'après-midi;
~**shave** l'après-rasage
age l'âge
agency l'agence
AIDS Déficience le Syndrome
d'immunodéficience acquise
air l'air; ~ **conditioning** la
climatisation; ~ **pump** la pompe
à air; ~**line** la compagnie
aérienne; ~**mail** par avion;
~**plane** l'avion; ~**port** l'aéroport
aisle (plane) le couloir;
~ **(theater)** l'allée; ~ **seat** le
siège couloir
allergic allergique; ~ **reaction**
la réaction allergique
allow v permettre
alone seul

alter v modifier
alternate route la route
différente
aluminum foil le papier
aluminium
amazing surprenant
ambulance l'ambulance
American américain
amusement park le parc
d'attractions
anemic anémique
anesthesia l'anesthésie
animal l'animal
ankle la cheville
antibiotic l'antibiotique
antiques store l'antiquaire
antiseptic cream la crème
antiseptique
anything rien
apartment l'appartement
appendix (body part) l'appendice
appetizer l'entrée
appointment le rendez-vous
arcade la salle de jeux
area code le code régional
arm le bras
aromatherapy l'aromathérapie
around (the corner) au coin
arrivals (airport) les arrivées
arrive v arriver
artery l'artère
arthritis l'arthrite
art l'art
Asian asiatique

adj adjective	**BE** British English	v verb
adv adverb	n noun	

aspirin l'aspirine
asthmatic asthmatique
ATM le distributeur automatique de billets; **~ card** la carte de retrait
attack l'attaque
attend *v* participer
attraction (place) le lieu touristique
attractive beau
Australia l'Australie
Australian australien
automatic automatique; **~ car** la voiture automatique
available disponible

B

baby le bébé; **~ bottle** le biberon; **~ wipe** la lingette pour bébé; **~sitter** le baby-sitter
back (body part) le dos; **~ache** le mal de dos; **~pack** le sac à dos
bag le sac
baggage [BE] le bagage; **~ claim** le retrait des bagages; **~ ticket** l'étiquette
bakery la boulangerie
ballet le ballet
bandage le pansement
bank la banque
bar (place) le bar
barbecue le barbecue
barber le coiffeur pour hommes
baseball le baseball
basket (grocery store) le panier

basketball le basketball
bathroom la salle de bains
battery la pile
battleground le champ de bataille
be *v* être
beach la plage
beautiful beau
bed le lit; **~ and breakfast** le bed and breakfast
before avant
begin *v* commencer
beginner le débutant
behind derrière
beige beige
belt la ceinture
berth la couchette
best meilleur
better mieux
bicycle la bicyclette; le vélo
big grand **~ bigger** plus grand
bike route la piste cyclable
bikini le bikini; **~ wax** l'épilation à la cire du maillot
bill (charge) *v* facturer; **~** *n* **(invoice)** la facture; **~** *n* **(money)** la coupure; **~** *n* **(of sale)** le reçu
bird l'oiseau
birthday l'anniversaire
black noir
bladder la vessie
bland sans goût
blanket la couverture
bleed *v* saigner
blood le sang; **~ pressure** la tension
blouse le chemisier

blue bleu
board *v* embarquer; ~**ing pass** la carte d'embarquement
boat le bateau
bone l'os
book le livre; ~**store** la librairie
boots les bottes
boring ennuyant
botanical garden le jardin botanique
bother *v* ennuyer
bottle la bouteille; ~ **opener** l'ouvre-bouteille
bowl le saladier
box la boîte
boxing match le match de boxe
boy le garçon; ~**friend** le petit-ami
bra le soutien-gorge
bracelet le bracelet
brakes (car) les freins
break *v* **(tooth/bone)** casser
breakdown la panne
breakfast le petit déjeuner
break-in (burglary) l'effraction
breast le sein; ~**feed** *v* allaiter
breathe *v* respirer
bridge pont
briefs (clothing) les slips
bring *v* apporter
British anglais
broken cassé
brooch la broche
broom le balai
brother le frère
brown marron
bug l'insecte

building le bâtiment
burn *v* brûler
bus le bus; ~ **station** la gare routière; ~ **stop** l'arrêt de bus; ~ **ticket** le ticket de bus; ~ **tour** la visite en bus
business les affaires; ~ **card** la carte de visite; ~ **center** le centre d'affaires; ~ **class** la classe affaire; ~ **hours** les heures d'ouverture
butcher le boucher
buttocks les fesses
buy *v* acheter
bye au revoir

C

cabaret le cabaret
cabin la cabine
cable car le téléphérique
café le café
call *v* appeler; ~ **collect** appeler ~ *n* l'appel en PCV;
calories les kilocalories
camera l'appareil photo; ~ **case** le sac à appareil photo; ~ **store** la boutique photo
camp *v* camper; ~**ing stove** le réchaud; ~**site** le camping
can opener le l'ouvre-boîte
Canada le Canada
Canadian canadien
cancel *v* annuler
candy le bonbon
canned goods les conserves

canyon la gorge
car la voiture; ~ hire [BE] la voiture de location; ~ park [BE] le parking; rental ~ la voiture de location; ~ seat le siège bébé
carafe la carafe
card la carte; ATM ~ la carte de retrait; credit ~ la carte de crédit; phone ~ le carte de téléphone
carry-on (piece of hand luggage) le bagage à main
cart le chariot
carton le paquet; ~ of cigarettes la cartouche de cigarettes
case (amount) le cas
cash v encaisser; ~ n le liquide; ~ advance l'avance
cashier la caisse
casino le casino
castle le château
cathedral la cathédrale
cave la grotte
CD le CD (disque compact)
cell phone le portable
Celsius Celsius
centimeter le centimètre
certificate le certificat
chair la chaise; ~ lift le télésiège
change v (baby) changer; ~ (money) échanger; ~ n (money) la monnaie
charcoal le charbon de bois
charge v (credit card) payer par carte

charge (cost) le coût
cheap bon marché
cheaper moins cher
check v (luggage) enregistrer; ~ (on something) vérifier; ~ n (payment) le chèque; ~-in (hotel/airport) l'enregistrement; ~ing account le compte courant; ~-out (hotel) quitter la chambre
Cheers! Santé!
chemical toilet les toilettes portables
chemist [BE] la pharmacie
cheque [BE] le chèque
chest (body part) la poitrine; ~ pain la douleur à la poitrine
chewing gum le chewing-gum
child l'enfant; ~'s seat le siège enfant
children's menu le menu enfant
children's portion la portion enfant
chopsticks les baguettes
church l'église
cigar le cigare
cigarette la cigarette
class la classe
classical music la musique classique
clean v nettoyer; ~ adj propre; ~ing product le produit d'entretien; ~ing supplies les produits d'entretien
clear v (on an ATM) effacer
cliff la falaise

cling film [BE] le cellophane

close v (shop) fermer;
~ adv près; ~d fermé

clothing les vêtements;
~ store le magasin de
vêtements

club le club

coat le manteau

coffee shop le café

coin la pièce

colander la passoire

cold (sickness) le rhume;
~ (temperature) froid

colleague le collègue

cologne l'eau de Cologne

color la couleur

comb le peigne

come v venir

complaint la plainte

computer l'ordinateur

concert le concert; ~ hall
la salle de concert

condition (medical)
l'état de santé

conditioner l'après-shampooing

condom le préservatif

conference la conférence

confirm v confirmer

congestion la congestion

connect v (internet)
se connecter

connection (flight)
la correspondance;
~ (internet) la connexion

constipated constipé

consulate le consulat

consultant le consultant

contact v contacter

contact lens les lentilles de
contact; ~ solution
la solution pour lentilles
de contact

contagious contagieux

convention hall le palais des
congrès

conveyor belt le carrousel

cook v cuisiner; ~ing gas
le gaz

cool (temperature) frais

copper le cuivre

corkscrew le tire-bouchon

cost v coûter

cot le lit pliant

cotton le coton

cough v tousser; ~ n la toux

country code le code national

cover charge (bar, club) le droit
d'entrée; ~ (restaurant)
le couvert

crash v (car) avoir un
accident

cream (ointment) la crème

credit card la carte de crédit

crew neck le col rond

crib le berceau

crystal le cristal

cup la tasse

currency la monnaie;
~ exchange l'échange de
monnaie; ~ exchange office
le bureau de change

current account [BE] le compte
courant

customs la douane

cut v couper; ~ n (injury)
la coupure

cute mignon
cycling faire du vélo

D

damage v abîmer;
~**d** endommagé
dance v danser; ~ **club** la
discothèque; ~**ing** dansant
dangerous dangereux
dark sombre
date (calendar) la date
day le jour
deaf sourd
debit card la carte de retrait
deck chair la chaise longue
declare v déclarer
decline v **(credit card)** refuser
deeply profondément
degree (temperature) le degré
delay v retarder
delete v **(computer)** supprimer
delicatessen la charcuterie
delicious délicieux
denim jean
dentist le dentiste
denture le dentier
deodorant le déodorant
department store le grand
magasin
departures (airport) les départs
deposit v déposer; ~ **(bank)**
le dépôt
desert le désert
detergent le détergent
develop v **(film)** développer
diabetic diabétique

dial v composer
diamond le diamant
diaper la couche
diarrhea la diarrhée
diesel le gazole
difficult difficile
digital numérique; ~ **camera**
l'appareil photo numérique;
~ **photo** la photo numérique
dining room la salle à manger
dinner le dîner
direction la direction
dirty sale
disabled [BE] handicapé;
~ **accessible [BE]** accessible
aux handicapés
disconnect v **(computer)**
déconnecter
discount la réduction
dish (kitchen) la vaisselle;
~**washer** le lave-vaisselle;
~**washing liquid** le détergent
pour lave-vaisselle
display montrer; ~ **case**
la vitrine
disposable jetable; ~ **razor**
le rasoir jetable
dive v plonger; ~**ing equipment**
l'équipement de plongée
divorce v divorcer
dizzy avoir des vertiges
doctor le docteur
doll la poupée
dollar (U.S.) le dollar
domestic national;
~ **flight** le vol national
door la porte
dormitory le dortoir

double bed le lit double

downtown (direction) vers le centre-ville; ~ **area** le centre-ville

dozen la douzaine

drag lift le remonte-pentes

dress (piece of clothing) la robe; ~ **code** la tenue exigée

drink v boire; ~ n la boisson; ~ **menu** la carte des boissons

drinking water l'eau potable

drive v conduire; ~r's **license number** le numéro de permis de conduire

drop (medicine) la goutte

drowsiness la somnolence

dry cleaner la teinturerie

dubbed doublé

during pendant

duty (tax) la taxe

duty-free hors taxe

DVD DVD

E

ear l'oreille; ~**ache** l'otite

early tôt

earrings les boucles d'oreille

east est

easy facile

eat v manger

economy class la classe économique

elbow le coude

electric outlet la prise électrique

elevator l'ascenseur

e-mail v envoyer un mail; ~ n le mail; ~ **address** l'adresse mail

emergency l'urgence; ~ **exit** la sortie de secours

empty v vider

enamel (jewelry) l'émail

end v finir

English anglais

engrave v graver

enjoy v prendre plaisir

enter v entrer

entertainment le divertissement

entrance l'entrée

envelope l'enveloppe

equipment l'équipement

escalators l'escalator

e-ticket le billet électronique

EU resident le résident européen

euro l'euro

evening la soirée

excess l'excès

exchange v échanger; ~ n (place) le bureau de change; ~ **rate** le taux de change

excursion l'excursion

excuse v excuser

exhausted épuisé

exit v sortir; ~ n la sortie

expensive cher

expert (skill level) l'expert

exposure (film) la pose

express express; ~ **bus** le bus direct; ~ **train** l'express

extension (phone) le poste
extra extra; **~ large** très grand
extract v (tooth) arracher
eye l'œil
eyebrow wax l'épilation à la cire des sourcils

F

face le visage
facial le soin du visage
family la famille
fan (appliance) le ventilateur; **~** (souvenir) l'éventail
far loin
farm la ferme
far-sighted presbyte
fast vite; **~ food** le fast food
faster plus vite
fat free 0% de matières grasses
father le père
fax v envoyer un fax; n le fax; **~ number** le numéro de fax
feed v nourrir
ferry le ferry
fever la fièvre
field (sports) le terrain de sport
fill v faire le plein
fill v **out** (form) remplir
filling (tooth) le plombage
film (camera) la pellicule
fine (fee for breaking law) la contravention
finger le doigt; **~nail** l'ongle
fire le feu; **~ department** les pompiers; **~ door** la porte coupe-feu

first premier; **~ class** la première classe
fitting room la cabine d'essayage
fix v (repair) réparer
flashlight la lampe torche
flat tire [tyre BE] le pneu crevé
flight le vol
floor le sol
flower la fleur
folk music la musique folklorique
food la nourriture
foot le pied
football [BE] le football; **~ game** [BE] le match de football
for pour
forecast la météo
forest la forêt
fork la fourchette
form le formulaire
formula (baby) le lait pour bébés
fort le fort
fountain la fontaine
France la France
free libre
freezer le congélateur
French français
fresh frais
friend l'ami
frying pan la poêle
full-service le service complet
full-time le temps plein

G

game le match
garage le garage
garbage bag le sac poubelle
gas l'essence; ~ **station** la station service
gate (airport) la porte
gay gay; ~ **bar** le bar gay; ~ **club** le club gay
gel (hair) le gel
get off *v* **(a train, bus, subway)** descendre
get to *v* aller
gift le cadeau; ~ **shop** la boutique cadeaux
girl la fille; ~**friend** la petite-amie
give *v* donner
glass le verre;
glasses les lunettes
go *v* **(somewhere)** aller
gold l'or
golf course le terrain de golf
golf tournament le tournoi de golf
good *adj* bon; ~ *n* le produit; ~ **afternoon** bon après-midi; ~ **evening** bonsoir; ~ **morning** bonjour; ~**bye** au revoir
goods les produits
gram le gramme
grandchild les petits-enfants
grandparent les grands-parents
gray gris
green vert
grocery store le magasin de fruits et légumes
ground floor le rez-de-chaussée
groundcloth le tapis de sol

groundsheet le drap du dessous
group le groupe
guide le guide; ~ **book** le guide; ~ **dog** le chien d'aveugle
gym la gym
gynecologist le gynécologue

H

hair les cheveux; **dryer** le sèche-cheveux d'étudiant; ~ **salon** le coiffeur; ~**brush** la brosse; ~**cut** la coupe de cheveux; ~**spray** la laque; ~**style** le style de coiffure; ~**stylist** le coiffeur
half la moitié; ~ **hour** la demi-heure ~-**kilo** le demi-kilo
hammer le marteau
hand la main; ~ **luggage [BE]** le bagage à main; ~**bag [BE]** le sac à main
handicapped l'handicapé; ~-**accessible** accessible aux handicapés
hangover la gueule de bois
happy heureux
hat le chapeau
have *v* avoir
head (body part) la tête; ~**ache** le mal de tête; ~**phones** les écouteurs
health la santé; ~ **food store** le magasin de produits diététiques
heart le cœur; ~ **condition** le problème cardiaque

heat le chauffage; **~er**
le chauffage
hectare l'hectare
hello bonjour
helmet le casque
help v aider; **~** n l'aide
here ici
hi salut
high haut; **~chair** la chaise
haute; **~-heeled shoes** les
chaussures à talons aiguilles;
~way l'autoroute
hiking boots les chaussures de
marche
hill la colline
hire v [BE] louer; **~ car** [BE]
la voiture de location
hitchhike v faire de l'auto-stop
hockey le hockey
holiday [BE] les vacances
horsetrack le champ de course
hospital l'hôpital
hostel l'auberge de jeunesse
hot (spicy) épicé;
~ (temperature) chaud;
~ spring la source chaude;
~ water l'eau chaude
hotel l'hôtel
hour l'heure
house la maison; **~hold
goods** les produits ménagers;
~keeping service le service
d'entretien
how comment; **~ much** combien
hug v enlacer
hungry faim
hurt la douleur
husband le mari

I

ibuprofen l'ibuprofène
ice la glace; **~ hockey**
le hockey sur glace
icy glacé
identification l'identification
ill malade
in dans
include v inclure
indoor pool la piscine intérieure
inexpensive pas cher
infected infecté
information (phone) les
renseignements; **~ desk**
le bureau des renseignements
insect l'insecte; **~ bite**
la piqûre d'insecte; **~ repellent**
la lotion anti-insectes
insert v insérer
insomnia l'insomnie
instant message le message
instantané
insulin l'insuline
insurance l'assurance;
~ card la carte d'assurance;
~ company la compagnie
d'assurance
interesting intéressant
intermediate le niveau
intermédiaire
international (airport area)
l'international (terminal);
~ flight le vol international;
~ student card la carte
internationale d'étudiant

internet l'internet; ~ **cafe** le cyber café; ~ **service** le service internet
interpreter l'interprète
intersection l'intersection
intestine l'intestin
introduce v présenter
invoice [BE] la facture
Ireland l'Irlande
Irish irlandais
iron v repasser; ~ n (clothes) le fer à repasser
Italian italien

J

jacket la veste
jar le pot
jaw la mâchoire
jazz le jazz; ~ **club** le club de jazz
jeans le jean
jet ski le jet ski
jeweler la bijouterie
jewelry le bijou
join v joindre
joint (body part) l'articulation

K

key la clé; ~ **card** la carte de la chambre; ~ **ring** la chaîne
kiddie pool la pataugeoire
kidney (body part) le rein
kilo le kilo; ~**gram** le kilogramme; ~**meter** le kilomètre

kiss v embrasser
kitchen la cuisine; ~ **foil [BE]** le papier aluminium
knee le genou
knife le couteau

L

lace la dentelle
lactose intolerant allergique au lactose
lake le lac
large grand
larger plus grand
last dernier
late (time) tard
later plus tard
laundromat la laverie automatique
laundry la lessive; ~ **facility** la buanderie; ~ **service** le service de nettoyage
lawyer l'avocat
leather le cuir
leave v partir
left (direction) à gauche
leg la jambe
lens le verre
less moins
lesson la leçon
letter la lettre
library la bibliothèque
life jacket le gilet de sauvetage
lifeguard le secouriste
lift [BE] l'ascenseur; ~ **pass** le forfait

light (cigarette) v allumer;
~ adj (overhead) blond;
~bulb l'ampoule
lighter le briquet
like v aimer
line (train) la ligne
linen le lin
lip les lèvres
liquor store le marchand de
vins et de spiritueux
liter le litre
little adv peu; ~ adj petit
live v vivre
liver (body part) le foie
loafers les mocassins
local du quartier
lock v fermer; ~ n le cadenas;
~er la consigne
log off (computer) terminer
une session
log on (computer) ouvrir une
session
long long; ~ sleeves les
manches longues; ~-sighted
[BE] presbyte
look v regarder
lose v (something) perdre
lost perdu; ~ and found les
objets trouvés
lotion la crème
louder plus fort
love v (someone) aimer;
~ n amour
low bas
luggage le bagage; ~ cart le
chariot; ~ locker la consigne;
~ ticket le retrait des bagages

lunch le déjeuner
lung le poumon

M

magazine le magazine
magnificent magnifique
mail le courrier; ~box
la boîte-à-lettres
main attraction la principale
attraction touristique
main course le plat principal
mall le centre commercial
man l'homme
manager le responsable
manicure la manucure
manual car la voiture manuelle
map la carte
market le marché
married marié
marry v se marier
mass (church service) la messe
massage le massage
match le match
meal le repas
measure v (someone)
mesurer
measuring cup la mesure
measuring spoon la cuillère à
doser
mechanic le mécanicien
medicine le médicament
medium (size) moyen
meet v (someone) rencontrer
meeting la réunion; ~ room
la salle de réunion

membership card la carte de membre
memorial (place) le lieu commémoratif
memory card la carte mémoire
mend v raccourcir
menstrual cramp les règles douloureuses
menu la carte
message le message
meter (parking) l'horodateur
microwave le micro-onde
midday [BE] midi
midnight minuit
mileage le kilométrage
mini-bar le mini bar
minute la minute
missing disparu
mistake l'erreur
mobile home le mobile home
mobile phone [BE] le portable
mobility la mobilité
money l'argent
month le mois
mop la serpillière
moped la mobylette
more plus
morning le matin
mosque la mosquée
mother la mère
motion sickness (air) le mal de l'air; ~ (sea) le mal de mer
motor boat le bateau à moteur
motorcycle la mobylette
motorway [BE] l'autoroute
mountain la montagne
mousse la mousse

mouth la bouche
movie le film; ~ theater le cinéma
mug v attaquer
muscle le muscle
museum le musée
music la musique; ~ store le disquaire

N

nail file la lime á ongle
nail salon l'onglerie
name le nom
napkin la serviette
nappies [BE] les couches
nationality la nationalité
nature preserve la réserve naturelle
nausea la nausée
near près; ~by près de; ~-sighted myope
neck le cou
necklace le collier
need v avoir besoin
newspaper le journal
newsstand le kiosque à journaux
next suivant
nice bien
night la nuit
nightclub le night club
no non
non-alcoholic non alcoolisé
non-smoking non fumeur
noon midi
north nord

nose le nez
note [BE] la coupure
nothing rien
notify *v* informer
novice (skill level) novice
now maintenant
number le nombre; le numéro
nurse l'infirmier

O

office le bureau; ~ hours les
heures d'ouverture
off-licence [BE] le marchand de
vins et de spiritueux
oil l'huile
OK d'accord
old vieux
on the corner au coin
once une fois
one un; ~-way (ticket) l'aller
simple; ~-way street le sens
unique
only seulement
open *v* ouvrir; ~ *adj* ouvert
opera l'opéra; ~ house l'opéra
opposite le contraire
optician l'opticien
orange (color) orange
orchestra l'orchestre
order *v* commander
outdoor pool la piscine extérieure
outside dehors
over-the-counter
(medication) sans ordonnance
overlook (scenic place) le point
d'observation

overnight de nuit
oxygen treatment le soin à
l'oxygène

P

pacifier la tétine
pack *v* faire les bagages
package le colis
pad [BE] la serviette hygiénique
pain la douleur
pajamas le pyjama
palace le palais
panties les culottes
pants le pantalon
pantyhose le collant
paper le papier; ~ towel
la serviette en papier
paracetamol [BE]
le paracétamol
park *v* se garer; ~ *n* le parc;
~ing garage le garage;
~ing lot le parking
part (for car) la pièce; ~-time
le temps partiel
pass through *v* passer
passenger le passager
passport le passeport;
~ control le contrôle de
passeport
password le mot de passe
pastry shop la pâtisserie
path le chemin
pay *v* payer; ~ phone le
téléphone public
peak (of a mountain)
le sommet

pearl la perle
pedestrian le piéton
pediatrician le pédiatre
pedicure la pédicure
pen le stylo
penicillin la pénicilline
penis le pénis
per par; ~ day par jour; ~ hour
par heure; ~ night par nuit;
~ week par semaine
perfume le parfum
period (menstrual) les règles;
~ (of time) la période
permit v permettre
personal identification number
(PIN) le code secret
petite menue
petrol [BE] le l'essence;
~ station [BE] la station service
pewter l'étain
pharmacy la pharmacie
phone v téléphoner; ~ n le
téléphone; ~ call l'appel;
~ card la carte de téléphone;
~ number le numéro de
téléphone
photo la photo; ~copy
la photocopie; ~graphy
la photographie
pick up v (something) prendre
picnic area l'aire de
pique-nique
piece le morceau
Pill (birth control) la pilule
pillow l'oreiller
pink rose
piste [BE] la piste;
~ map [BE] la carte des pistes

pizzeria la pizzeria
place v (a bet) parier
plane l'avion
plastic wrap le cellophane
plate l'assiette
platform le quai
platinum platine
play v jouer; ~ n (theater)
la pièce ~ground l'aire de jeux
~pen le parc
please s'il vous plaît
pleasure le plaisir
plunger le déboucheur de
toilettes
plus size grande taille
pocket la poche
poison le poison
poles (skiing) les bâtons
police la police; ~ report
le rapport de police; ~ station
le commissariat de police
pond l'étang
pool la piscine
pop music la pop musique
portion la portion
post [BE] le courrier;
~ office le bureau de
poste; ~box [BE]
la boîte-à-lettres; ~card
la carte postale
pot la casserole
pottery la poterie
pound (British sterling) la livre
sterling
pregnant enceinte
prescribe v prescrire
prescription l'ordonnance
press v (clothing) repasser

price le prix
print v imprimer
problem le problème
produce v produire;
  ~ store le marchand de fruits
  et légumes
prohibit v interdire
pronounce v prononcer
public public
pull v (door sign) tirer
purple pourpre
purse le sac
push v (door sign) pousser
pushchair [BE] la poussette

Q

quality la qualité
question la question
quiet le silence; le calme

R

racetrack la piste de courses
racket (sports) la raquette
railway station [BE] la gare
rain la pluie;
  ~coat l'imperméable;
  ~forest la forêt vierge
rainy pluvieux
rap (music) le rap
rape v violer; ~ n le viol
rash l'irritation cutanée
razor blade la lame de rasoir
reach v atteindre
ready prêt
real vrai

receipt le reçu
receive v recevoir
reception la réception
recharge v recharger
recommend v recommander
recommendation
  la recommandation
recycling les ordures à recycler
red rouge
refrigerator le réfrigérateur
region la région
registered mail le courrier
  recommandé
regular ordinaire
relationship la relation
rent v louer; **~al car** la voiture
  de location
repair v réparer
repeat v répéter
reservation la réservation;
  ~ desk le bureau de
  réservation
reserve v réserver
restaurant le restaurant
restroom les toilettes
retired v prendre sa retraite
return v (something) rendre;
  ~ n [BE] l'aller-retour
rib (body part) la côte
right (direction) à droite;
  ~ of way le droit de
  passage
ring la bague
river la rivière
road map la carte routière
rob v voler
romantic romantique

room la pièce; ~ key la clé;
~ service le service de
chambre
round-trip l'aller-retour
route la route
rowboat la barque
rubbish [BE] les poubelles;
~ bag [BE] le sac poubelle
rugby le rugby
ruins les ruines

S

sad triste
safe *adj* en sécurité;
~ *n* le coffre-fort
sales tax la TVA
same le même
sandals les sandales
sanitary napkin la serviette
hygiénique
saucepan la casserole
sauna le sauna
save *v* (computer) sauvegarder
savings (account) le compte
épargne
scanner scanner
scarf l'écharpe
schedule *v* prévoir;
~ *n* l'horaire
science la science
scissors les ciseaux
sea la mer
seat le siège
security la sécurité
see *v* voir
self-service le self-service

sell *v* vendre
seminar le séminaire
send *v* envoyer
senior citizens les seniors
separated (marriage)
séparés
serious sérieux
service (in a restaurant)
le service
sexually transmitted
disease (STD) les maladies
sexuellement transmissibles
shampoo le shampooing
sharp tranchant
shaving cream la mousse à
raser
sheet le drap
shirt la chemise
ship *v* envoyer
shoe store le magasin de
chaussures
shoes les chaussures
shop *v* faire des achats
shopping les courses;
~ area le quartier des
magasins; ~ centre [BE]
le centre commercial; ~ mall
le centre commercial
short court; ~-sighted
[BE] myope; ~ sleeves
les manches courtes; ~s
le short
shoulder l'épaule
show *v* montrer
shower la douche
shrine le lieu saint
sick malade
side dish l'accompagnement

side effect l'effet secondaire
sightseeing le tourisme;
~ **tour** la visite touristique
sign v signer
silk la soie
single (unmarried) adj célibataire;
n ~ **bed** le lit une place;
~ **prints** le tirage unique;
~ **room** la chambre simple
sink l'évier
sister la sœur
sit v s'asseoir
size la taille
ski v skier; ~ n le ski;
~ **lift** le télésiège
skin la peau
skirt la jupe
sleep v dormir
sleeper car le wagon
couchette
sleeping bag le sac de
couchage
sleeping car [BE] le wagon
couchette
slice la tranche
slippers les chaussons
slower plus lent
slowly lentement
small petit
smaller plus petit
smoke v fumer
smoking (area) la zone
fumeur
snack bar le bar
sneakers les tennis
snorkeling equipment
l'équipement de plongée
snowboard le snowboard

snowshoe la chaussure de ski
snowy neigeux
soap le savon
soccer le football; ~ **game**
le match de football
sock la chaussette
soother [BE] la tétine
sore throat le mal de gorge
sorry désolé
south sud
souvenir le souvenir; ~ **store**
le magasin de souvenirs
spa le spa
spatula la spatule
speak v parler
special (food) la spécialité; le
plat typique
specialist (doctor)
le spécialiste
specimen l'échantillon
speed (velocity) la vitesse
spell v épeler
spicy épicé
spine (body part) la colonne
vertébrale
spoon la cuillère
sporting goods store
le magasin de sport
sports le sport; ~ **massage**
le massage sportif
sprain l'entorse
stadium le stade
stairs les escaliers
stamp v (a ticket) timbrer;
~ n (postage) le timbre
start v (a car) démarrer; v
(to begin) commencer
starter [BE] l'entrée

station la station; ~ wagon le break; bus ~ la gare routière; gas ~ la station service; muster ~ [BE] la salle d'attente; petrol ~ [BE] la station service; subway ~ la station de métro; train ~ la gare

statue la statue

stay v rester

steal v voler

steep escarpé

sterling silver l'argent fin

sting la piqûre

stolen volé

stomach l'estomac; ~ache les maux de ventre

stop v arrêter; ~ n l'arrêt

store directory le plan du magasin

stove la gazinière

straight droit

strange étrange

stream le ruisseau

stroller la poussette

student l'étudiant

study v étudier

stunning stupéfiant

subtitle subtil

subway le métro; ~ station la station de métro

suit le costume; ~case la valise

sun le soleil; ~ block l'écran solaire; ~burn le coup de soleil; ~glasses les lunettes de soleil

sunny ensoleillé

sunscreen la crème solaire

sunstroke l'insolation

super (fuel) le super; ~market le supermarché; ~vision la supervision

surfboard le surf

swallow v avaler

sweater le pull

sweatshirt le sweat-shirt

sweet (taste) sucré

sweets [BE] les bonbons

swell v gonfler

swim v nager

swimsuit le maillot de bain

symbol (keyboard) le symbole

synagogue la synagogue

T

table la table

tablet (medicine) le cachet

take v prendre

take away [BE] à emporter

tampon le tampon

taste v goûter

taxi le taxi

team l'équipe

teaspoon la cuillère à café

telephone le téléphone

temple (religious) le temple

temporary temporaire

tennis le tennis

tent la tente; ~ peg le piquet; ~ pole le pilier

terminal (airport) le terminal

terracotta la terre cuite

terrible terrible

text *v* (send a message) écrire;
~ *n* (message) le texte
thank *v* remercier; ~ **you** merci
that ça/cela
theater le théâtre
theft le vol
there là
thief le voleur
thigh la cuisse
thirsty soif
this ceci
throat la gorge
ticket le billet; ~ **office** la
billetterie
tie (clothing) la cravate
time le temps; ~**table** [BE] les
horaires
tire [tyre BE] le pneu
tired fatigué
tissues les Kleenex
to go aller
tobacconist le tabac
today aujourd'hui
toe l'orteil; ~**nail** l'ongle
toilet [BE] les toilettes;
~ **paper** le papier toilette
tomorrow demain
tongue la langue
tonight ce soir
too trop
tooth la dent; ~**paste**
le dentifrice
total (amount) le total
tough (food) dur
tour la visite
tourist le touriste;
~ **information office**
le syndicat d'initiative

tow truck la dépanneuse
towel la serviette
tower la tour
town la ville; ~ **hall** la mairie;
~ **map** la carte de la ville;
~ **square** le centre ville
toy le jouet; ~ **store** le magasin
de jouets
track (train) le quai
traditional traditionnel
traffic light le feu tricolore
trail la piste; ~ **map** la carte
des pistes
trailer la remorque
train le train; ~ **station** la gare
translate *v* traduire
trash les poubelles
travel *v* voyager; ~ **agency**
l'agence de voyage; ~ **sickness**
le mal des transports; ~**er's**
check [cheque BE] le chèque
de voyages
tree l'arbre
trim (hair cut) *v* égaliser
trip le voyage
trolley [BE] le chariot
trousers [BE] le pantalon
T-shirt le t-shirt
turn off *v* (lights) éteindre
turn on *v* (lights) allumer
TV la télé
type *v* taper

U

ugly laid
umbrella le parapluie
unattended sans surveillance

unbranded medication [BE] le médicament générique

unconscious inconscient

underground [BE] le métro; **~ station [BE]** la station de métro

underpants [BE] les slips

understand *v* comprendre

underwear les sous-vêtements

United Kingdom (U.K.) le Royaume Uni

United States (U.S.) les États-Unis

university l'université

unleaded (gas) sans plomb

upper supérieur

urgent urgent

use *v* utiliser

username le nom de l'utilisateur

utensil l'ustensile

V

vacancy libre

vacation les vacances

vaccination la vaccination

vacuum cleaner l'aspirateur

vagina le vagin

vaginal infection l'infection vaginale

valid valide

valley la vallée

valuable précieux

value la valeur

VAT [BE] la TVA

vegetarian végétarien

vehicle registration la carte grise

viewpoint [BE] le point d'observation

village le village

vineyard le vignoble

visit *v* visiter; **~ing hours** les heures de visite

visually impaired le malvoyant

vitamin la vitamine

V-neck le col en V

volleyball game le match de volleyball

vomit *v* vomir

W

wait *v* attendre; **~** *n* l'attente

waiter le serveur

waiting room la salle d'attente

waitress la serveuse

wake *v* réveiller; **~-up call** *n* l'appel réveil

walk *v* marcher; **~** *n* la promenade; **~ing route** le chemin de randonnée

wall clock la pendule

wallet le portefeuille

warm (something) *v* réchauffer **~** *adj* **(temperature)** chaud

washing machine la machine à laver

watch la montre

water skis les skis nautiques

waterfall la cascade

weather le temps

week la semaine; **~week-end** le week-end

weekly hebdomadaire
welcome v accueillir
well-rested bien reposé
west ouest
what quoi
wheelchair la chaise roulante;
 ~ ramp la rampe d'accès
when quand
where où
white blanc; ~ gold l'or blanc
who qui
widow le veuf
wife l'épouse
window la fenêtre; ~ case le
 chambranle
windsurfer le véliplanchiste
wine list la carte des vins
wireless internet l'accès Wi-Fi
wireless phone le portable
with avec
withdraw v retirer
withdrawal (bank) le retrait
without sans

woman la femme
wool la laine
work v travailler
wrap v emballer
wrist le poignet
write v écrire

Y

year l'année
yellow jaune; ~ gold l'or jaune
yes oui
yesterday hier
you're welcome de rien
young jeune
youth hostel l'auberge de
 jeunesse

Z

zoo le zoo

French–English Dictionary

A

à droite right (direction)
à gauche left (direction)
l'abbaye abbey
abîmer *v* damage
accéder *v* access
accepter *v* accept
l'accès Wi-Fi wireless internet
accessible aux handicapés handicapped- [disabled- BE] accessible
l'accident accident
l'accompagnement side dish
d'accord OK
accueillir *v* welcome
acheter *v* buy
l'acuponcture acupuncture
l'adaptateur adapter
l'addition bill (check)
l'adresse address; ~ **mail** e-mail address
l'aéroport airport
les affaires business
l'âge age
l'agence agency; ~ **de voyage** travel agency
l'aide *n* help
aider *v* help
aimer *v* like (someone); ~ *v* love (someone)
l'aire de jeux playground; ~ **de sport** field (sports)
l'aire de pique-nique picnic area

allaiter *v* breastfeed
l'allée aisle (theater)
aller *v* go (somewhere)
l'aller simple one-way (ticket)
allergique allergic; ~ **au lactose** lactose intolerant
l'aller-retour round-trip [return BE]
allumer *v* light (cigarette); ~ *v* turn on (lights)
l'ambulance ambulance
américain American
l'ami friend
amour *n* love
l'ampoule lightbulb
anémique anemic
l'anesthésie anesthesia
anglais British; English
l'animal animal
l'année year
l'anniversaire birthday
annuler *v* cancel
l'antibiotique antibiotic
l'antiquaire antique store
l'appareil photo camera; ~ **numérique** digital camera
l'appartement apartment
l'appel phone call
appeler *v* call
l'appendice appendix (body part)
apporter *v* bring
après after
l'après after; ~-**midi** afternoon; ~-**rasage** aftershave; ~-**shampooing** conditioner
l'arbre tree

la salle de jeux arcade

l'argent money; ~ fin sterling silver

l'aromathérapie aromatherapy

arracher v extract (tooth)

l'arrêt n stop; ~ de bus bus stop

arrêter v stop

les arrivées arrivals (airport)

arriver v arrive

l'art arts

l'artère artery

l'arthrite arthritis

l'articulation joint (body part)

l'ascenseur elevator [lift BE]

asiatique Asian

l'aspirateur vacuum cleaner

l'aspirine aspirin

l'assiette plate

l'assurance insurance

asthmatique asthmatic

l'attaque attack

attaquer v mug

atteindre v reach

attendre v wait

l'attente n wait

au coin on/around the corner

au revoir goodbye

l'auberge de jeunesse youth hostel

aujourd'hui today

l'Australie Australia

australien Australian

automatique automatic

l'autoroute highway [motorway BE]

avaler v swallow

l'avance cash advance

avant before

avec with

l'avion airplane

l'avocat lawyer

avoir v have; ~ besoin v need; ~ des vertiges dizzy; ~ la nausée nauseous; ~ un accident v crash (car)

B

le baby-sitter babysitter

le bagage à main carry-on [piece of hand luggage BE]

le bagage luggage [baggage BE]

la bague ring

les baguettes chopsticks

le balai broom

le ballet ballet

la banque bank

le bar bar (place), snack bar; ~ gay gay bar

le barbecue barbecue

la barque rowboat

bas low

le baseball baseball

le basketball basketball

le bateau boat; ~ à moteur motor boat

le bâtiment building

les bâtons poles (skiing)

beau attractive, beautiful

le bébé baby

le bed and breakfast bed and breakfast

beige beige
belle pretty
le berceau crib
le biberon baby bottle
la bibliothèque library
la bicyclette bicycle
bien well; ~ reposé
well-rested
le bijou jewelry
la bijouterie jeweler
le bikini bikini
la billeterie ticket office;
~ électronique e-ticket
blanc white
bleu blue
boire v drink
la boisson n drink
la boîte box; ~~à-lettres
mailbox [postbox BE]
bon adj good; ~ après-midi
good afternoon;
~marché cheap
le bonbon candy [sweet BE]
bonjour hello, good
morning
bonsoir good evening
les bottes boots
la bouche mouth
le boucher butcher
les boucles d'oreille earrings
la boulangerie bakery
la bouteille bottle
la boutique photo camera store
le bracelet bracelet
le bras arm
le briquet lighter
la broche brooch
la brosse hairbrush

brûler v burn
la buanderie laundry facility
le bureau office; ~ de change
currency exchange office;
~ de poste post office;
~ des renseignements
information desk;
~ de réservation reservation
desk
le bus bus; ~ direct express
bus

C

ça that
le cabaret cabaret
la cabine cabin;
~ d'essayage fitting
[changing BE] room
le cachet tablet (medicine)
le cadeau gift
le cadenas n lock
le café café, coffee shop
la caisse cashier
les kilocalories calories
camper v camp
le camping campsite
le Canada Canada
canadien Canadian
la carafe carafe
le carrousel conveyor belt
la carte map, card;
~ d'assurance insurance card;
~ des boissons drink menu;
~ de la chambre key card;
~ de crédit credit card;
~ d'embarquement
boarding pass;

~ **internationale d'étudiant**
international student card;
~ **grise** vehicle registration;
~ **de membre** membership
card; ~ **mémoire** memory
card; ~ **des pistes** trail [piste
BE] map; ~ **postale** postcard;
~ **de retrait** ATM/debit card;
~ **routière** road map;
~ **de téléphone** phone card;
~ **de la ville** town map;
~ **de visite** business card
la carte des vins wine list
la cartouche (de cigarettes)
carton (of cigarettes)
le cas case (amount)
la cascade waterfall
le casino casino
le casque helmet
cassé broken
casser v break (tooth, bone)
la casserole pot, saucepan
la cathédrale cathedral
la cave cave, cellar (wine)
le CD (disque compact) CD
ce soir tonight
ceci this
la ceinture belt
cela that
célibataire single (unmarried)
le cellophane plastic wrap
[cling film BE]
Celsius Celsius
le centimètre centimeter
centre center; ~ **commercial**
shopping mall [centre BE];
~ **d'affaires** business center;
~ **ville** town square; ~**-ville**
downtown area

le certificat certificate
la chaîne key ring, chain
la chaise chair; ~ **haute**
highchair; ~ **longue** deck
chair; ~ **roulante** wheelchair
le chambranle display window/
case
la chambre simple single room
le champ field; ~ **de bataille**
battleground; ~ **la piste de
course** horsetrack
le change n exchange (place)
changer v change (baby)
le chapeau hat
le charbon de bois charcoal
la charcuterie delicatessen
le chariot cart [trolley BE]
le château castle
chaud hot, warm (temperature)
le chauffage heat (indoor)
le chauffage heater
la chaussette sock
les chaussons slippers
les chaussures shoes; ~ **de ski**
snowshoes; ~ **à talons aiguilles**
high-heeled shoes; ~ **de marche**
hiking boots; ~ **plates** flat shoes
le chemin trail, path;
~ **de randonnée** walking route
la chemise shirt
le chemisier blouse
le chèque n check [cheque BE]
(payment); ~ **de voyages**
traveler's check [cheque BE]
cher expensive
les cheveux hair
la cheville ankle
le chewing-gum chewing gum
le chien d'aveugle guide dog

chinois Chinese
le cigare cigar
la cigarette cigarette
le cinéma movie theater
les ciseaux scissors
la classe class; ~ **affaire** business class; ~ **économique** economy class
la clé key
la climatisation air conditioning
le club club; ~ **gay** gay club; ~ **de jazz** jazz club
le code code; ~ **national** country code; ~ **régional** area code; ~ **secret** personal identification number (PIN)
le cœur heart
le coffre-fort safe (receptacle)
le coiffeur hair salon
le coiffeur pour hommes barber
le col rond crew neck
le col en V V-neck
le colis package
le collègue colleague
le collier necklace
la colline hill
la colonne vertébrale spine (body part)
combien how much
commander v order
commencer v begin
comment how
le commissariat de police police station
la compagnie aérienne airline
la compagnie d'assurance insurance company

composer v dial
comprendre v understand
le compte account; ~ **courant** checking [current BE] account; ~ **épargne** savings account
le concert concert
conduire v drive
la conférence conference
confirmer v confirm
le congélateur freezer
la congestion congestion
se connecter v connect (internet)
la connexion connection (internet, telephone)
les conserves canned goods
la consigne luggage locker
la consigne locker
constipé constipated
le consulat consulate
le consultant consultant
contacter v contact
contagieux contagious
le contraire opposite
la contravention fine (fee for breaking law)
le contrôle de passeport passport control
la correspondance change (buses); ~ **connection** (flight); ~ v transfer (change trains/ flights)
le costume suit
la côte rib (body part)
le coton cotton
la couche diaper [nappy BE]
la couchette berth
le coude elbow

la couleur color
le couloir aisle (plane)
le cou neck
le coup de soleil sunburn
couper v cut
la coupure bill [note BE] (money); ~ cut (injury)
le courrier mail [post BE]; ~ recommandé registered mail
court short
le coût charge (cost)
le couteau knife
coûter v cost
le couvert cover charge (restaurant)
la couverture blanket
la cravate tie (clothing)
la crème cream/lotion; ~ antiseptique antiseptic cream; ~ solaire sunscreen
le cristal crystal
la cuillère spoon; ~ à café teaspoon; ~ à doser measuring spoon
le cuir leather
la cuisine kitchen
cuisiner v cook
la cuisse thigh
le cuivre copper
les culottes panties
le cyber café internet café

D

dangereux dangerous
dans in

dansant dancing
danser v dance
la date date (calendar)
de nuit overnight
de rien you're welcome
le déboucheur de toilettes plunger
le débutant beginner
déclarer v declare
décoller v take off (plane)
déconnecter disconnect (computer)
le degré degree (temperature)
dehors outside
le déjeuner lunch
délicieux delicious
demain tomorrow
démarrer v start (an automobile)
demi half; ~-heure half hour; ~-kilo half-kilo
la dent tooth
la dentelle lace
le dentier denture
le dentifrice toothpaste
le dentiste dentist
le déodorant deodorant
la dépanneuse tow truck
les départs departures (airport)
déposer v deposit
le dépôt deposit (bank)
dernier last
derrière behind
descendre v get off (a train, bus, subway)
le désert desert

désolé sorry
le détergent detergent;
~ **pour lave-vaisselle**
dishwashing liquid
développer v develop (film)
la déviation alternate route
diabétique diabetic
le diamant diamond
la diarrhée diarrhea
difficile difficult
dîner v dine; **le** ~ dinner
la direction direction
la discothèque dance club;
disparu missing
disponible available
le disquaire music store
**le distributeur automatique
de billets** automatic teller
machine (ATM)
le divertissement
entertainment
divorcer v divorce
le docteur doctor
le doigt finger
le dollar dollar (U.S.)
donner v give
dormir v sleep
le dortoir dormitory
le dos back (body part)
la douane customs
doublé dubbed
la douche shower
la douleur hurt, pain;
~ **à la poitrine** chest pain
la douzaine dozen
le drap sheet
droit straight; ~ **d'entrée** cover
charge (bar, club)

du quartier local
DVD DVD

E

l'eau water; ~ **chaude** hot
water; ~ **de Cologne** cologne;
~ **potable** drinking water
l'échange de monnaie currency
exchange
échanger v change (money)
l'échantillon specimen
l'écharpe scarf
l'école school
les écouteurs headphones
l'écran solaire sunblock
écrire v text (send a message);
~ v write
effacer v clear (on an ATM)
l'effet secondaire side effect
l'effraction break-in (burglary)
égaliser trim (hair cut)
l'église church
l'émail enamel (jewelry)
emballer v wrap
embarquer v board
embrasser v kiss
emporter to go [take away BE]
(food order)
en sécurité safe (protected)
encaisser v cash
enceinte pregnant
endommagé damaged
l'enfant child
enlacer v hug
ennuyant boring

l'enregistrement check-in
(hotel, airport)
enregistrer *v* check (luggage)
ensoleillé sunny
l'entorse sprain
l'entrée admission; ~ appetizer
[starter BE]; ~ entrance
entrer *v* enter
l'enveloppe envelope
envoyer *v* send, ship; ~ **un fax**
v fax; ~ **un mail** *v* e-mail
l'épaule shoulder
épeler *v* spell
épicé hot (spicy)
l'épilation à la cire du
maillot bikini wax
l'épilation à la cire des sourcils
eyebrow wax
épileptique epileptic
l'épouse wife
épuisé exhausted
l'équipe team
l'équipement equipment;
~ **de plongée** diving/
snorkeling equipment
l'erreur mistake
l'escalator escalators
les escaliers stairs
escarpé steep
ennuyer *v* bother
l'essence gas
l'essence petrol
est east
l'esthéticienne manicurist
l'estomac stomach
l'étain pewter
l'étang pond

l'état de santé condition
(medical); ~ **le problème**
cardiaque heart condition
les États-Unis United States (U.S.)
éteindre *v* turn off (lights)
l'étiquette baggage ticket
étrange strange
être *v* be
l'étudiant student
étudier *v* study
l'euro euro
l'éventail fan (souvenir)
l'évier sink
l'excès excess
l'excursion excursion
excuser *v* excuse
l'expert expert (skill level)
l'express express
l'express express train
extra extra

F

facile easy
la facture bill [invoice BE]
faim hungry
faire *v* make, do; ~ **des achats**
v shop; ~ **de l'auto stop**
v hitchhike; ~ **les bagages**
v pack; ~ **les courses**
shopping; ~ **le plein** *v* fill;
se ~ réveiller par téléphone
wake-up call; ~ **du**
tourisme sightseeing;
~ **du vélo** cycling;
~ **de la vitesse** speeding
faire un virement *v* transfer
(money)

la falaise cliff
la famille family
le fast-food fast food
fatigué tired
le fax fax
la femme woman
la fenêtre window
le fer à repasser *n* iron
  (clothes)
fermé closed
la ferme farm
fermer *v* close, lock
le ferry ferry
les fesses buttocks
le feu fire; ~ tricolore traffic
  light
fiancé engaged
la fièvre fever
la fille girl
le film movie
finir *v* end
la fleur flower
le foie liver (body part)
la fontaine fountain
le football soccer
  [football BE]
la forêt forest; ~ vierge
  rainforest
le forfait lift pass
le formulaire form
le fort fort
la fourchette fork
frais cool (temperature); ~ fresh
français French
la France France
les freins brakes (car)
le frère brother

froid cold (temperature)
fumer *v* smoke

G

le garage garage, parking garage
garer *v* park
le garçon boy
la gare train [railway BE] station
la gare routière bus station
gay gay
le gaz cooking gas
la gazinière stove
le gazole diesel
le gel gel (hair)
le genou knee
le gilet de sauvetage life jacket
glacé icy
la glace ice
gonfler *v* swell
la gorge canyon; ~ throat
goûter *v* taste
la goutte drop (medicine)
le gramme gram
grand large
le grand magasin department
  store
grande taille plus size
les grands-parents
  grandparent
graver *v* engrave
gris gray
le groupe group
la gueule de bois hangover
le guide guide, guidebook
la gym gym
le gynécologue gynecologist

H

l'handicapé handicapped
[disabled BE]
haut high
hebdomadaire weekly
l'hectare hectare
l'hétérosexuel heterosexual
l'heure hour
les heures d'ouverture
business/office hours
les heures de visite visiting hours
heureux happy
hier yesterday
le hockey hockey; ~ sur
glace ice hockey
l'homme man
l'hôpital hospital
l'horaire schedule [timetable BE]
hors taxe duty-free
l'hôtel hotel
l'huile oil

I

l'ibuprofène ibuprofen
ici here
l'identification identification
l'imperméable raincoat
imprimer v print
inclure v include
inconscient unconscious
infecté infected
l'infection vaginale vaginal
infection
l'infirmier nurse
informer v notify

l'insecte bug
insérer v insert
l'insolation sunstroke
l'insomnie insomnia
l'insuline insulin
interdire v prohibit
intéressant interesting
l'international (terminal)
international (airport area)
l'internet internet; ~ sans
fil wireless internet
l'interprète interpreter
l'intersection intersection
l'intestin intestine
irlandais Irish
l'Irlande Ireland
l'irritation cutanée rash
italien Italian

J

la jambe leg
le jardin botanique botanical
garden
jaune yellow
le jazz jazz
le jean jeans
jean denim
jetable disposable
le jeu game
jeune young
joindre v join
jouer v play
le jouet toy
le jour day
le journal newspaper
la jupe skirt

K

le kilo kilo; ~gramme
kilogram; ~métrage mileage;
~mètre kilometer; ~mètre
carré square kilometer
le kiosque à journaux newsstand
les Kleenex tissue

L

le lac lake
laid ugly
la laine wool
le lait pour bébés formula (baby)
la lame de rasoir razor blade
la lampe torche flashlight
la langue tongue
la laque hairspray
la laverie automatique
laundromat [launderette BE]
le lave-vaisselle dishwasher
la leçon lesson
lentement slowly
les lentilles de contact contact
lens
la lessive laundry
la lettre letter
les lèvres lip
la librairie bookstore
libre free; ~ vacancy
le lieu n place;
~ commémoratif memorial
(place); ~ saint shrine;
~ touristique attraction (place)
la ligne line (train)
la lime à ongle nail file
la lingette pour bébé baby wipe

le lin linen
le liquide n cash
le lit bed; ~ double double bed;
~ pliant cot
le litre liter
le livre book
la livre sterling pounds (British
sterling)
le logement accommodation
loin far
long long
la lotion anti-insectes
insect repellent
louer v rent [hire BE]
la lumière light (overhead)
les lunettes glasses;
~ de soleil sunglasses

M

la machine à laver washing
machine
la mâchoire jaw
le magasin store;
~ de chaussures shoe store;
~ de jouets toy store;
~ de produits diététiques
health food store;
~ de souvenirs souvenir store
~ de sport sporting goods
store; ~ de vêtements clothing
store; ~ de vins et spiritueux
liquor store
le magazine magazine
magnifique magnificent
le mail e-mail
le maillot de bain swimsuit
la main hand
maintenant now

la maison house

le mal sickness; ~ de l'air motion sickness (air); ~ de dos backache; ~ de gorge sore throat; ~ de mer motion sickness (sea); ~ de tête headache; ~ des transports travel sickness

malade ill, sick

les maladies sexuellement transmissibles sexually transmitted disease (STD)

malvoyant visually impaired

les manches courtes short sleeves

les manches longues long sleeves

manger v eat

le manteau coat

la manucure manicure

le marchand de fruits et légumes produce store

le marchand de vins et de spiritueux liquor store [off-licence BE]

le marché market

marcher v walk

le mari husband

marié married

la mairie town hall

se marier v marry

marron brown

le marteau hammer

le massage massage

le match n match; ~ de boxe boxing match; ~ de football soccer [football BE] game; ~ de volleyball volleyball game

le matin morning

le maux de ventre stomachache

le mécanicien mechanic

le médicament medicine

meilleur best

le même same

le menu menu; ~ enfant children's menu

la mer sea

merci thank you

la mère mother

le message message; ~ instantané instant message

la messe mass (church service)

la mesure measuring cup

mesurer to measure (someone)

la météo forecast

le mètre carré square meter

le métro subway [underground BE]

le micro-onde microwave

midi noon [midday BE]

mieux better

mignon cute

le mini bar mini-bar

minuit midnight

la minute minute

le mobile home mobile home

la mobilité mobility

la mobylette moped

les mocassins loafers

modifier v alter

moins less; ~ cher cheaper

le mois month

la moitié half

la monnaie n change (money); ~ currency

la **montagne** mountain
la **montre** watch
montrer v show
le **morceau** piece
la **mosquée** mosque
le **mot de passe** password
la **moto** motorcycle
la **mousse** mousse; ~ **à raser** shaving cream
moyen medium (size)
le **muscle** muscle
le **musée** museum
la **musique** music; ~ **classique** classical music; ~ **folklorique** folk music
myope near- [short- BE] sighted

nager v swim
national domestic
la **nationalité** nationality
neigeux snowy
nettoyer v clean
le **nez** nose
le **night club** nightclub
le **niveau intermédiaire** intermediate
noir black
le **nom** name; ~ **de l'utilisateur** username
non no; ~ **alcoolisé** non-alcoholic; ~ **fumeur** non-smoking
nord north
nourrir v feed
le **novice** novice (skill level)

de nuit overnight
la **nuit** night
numérique digital
le **numéro** number; ~ **de fax** fax number; ~ **de permis de conduire** driver's license number; ~ **de téléphone** phone number

les **objets trouvés** lost and found
l'**œil** eye
l'**oiseau** bird
l'**ongle** fingernail, toenail
l'**opéra** opera
l'**opticien** optician
l'**or** gold; ~ **blanc** white gold; ~ **jaune** yellow gold
orange orange (color)
l'**orchestre** orchestra
ordinaire regular
l'**ordinateur** computer
l'**ordonnance** prescription
les **ordures à recycler** recycling
l'**oreille** ear
l'**oreiller** pillow
l'**orteil** toe
l'**os** bone
l'**otite** earache
où where
ouest west
oui yes
ouvert open
l'**ouvre-bouteille/boîte** bottle/ can opener
ouvrir v open; ~ **une session** v log on (computer)

P

le palais palace
le palais des congrès
  convention hall
le panier basket (grocery store)
la panne breakdown
le pansement bandage
le pantalon pants [trousers BE]
le papier paper; ~ aluminium
  aluminum [kitchen BE] foil;
  ~ toilette toilet paper
le paquet carton
par by; ~ avion airmail; ~ heure
  per hour; ~ jour per day; ~ nuit
  per night; ~ semaine per week
le paracétamol acetaminophen
  [paracetamol BE]
le parapluie umbrella
le parc playpen; ~ park;
  ~ d'attractions amusement
  park
le parfum perfume
parier to place (a bet)
le parking parking lot
  [car park BE]
parler v speak
participer v attend
pas cher inexpensive
le passager passenger
le passeport passport
passer v pass through
la passoire colander
la pataugeoire kiddie pool
la pâtisserie pastry shop
payer v pay; ~ par carte
  v charge (credit card)
la peau skin

le pédiatre pediatrician
la pédicure pedicure
le peigne comb
la pellicule film (camera)
pendant during
la pendule wall clock
la pénicilline penicillin
le pénis penis
perdre v lose (something)
perdu lost
le père father
la période period (of time)
la perle pearl
permettre v allow
la perte discharge (bodily fluid)
petit small
le petit child, small;
  ~-ami boyfriend;
  ~-amie girlfriend;
  ~ déjeuner breakfast
les petits-enfants grandchildren
peu little
la pharmacie pharmacy
  [chemist BE]
la photo photo; ~copie
  photocopy; ~graphie
  photography; ~ numérique
  digital photo
la pièce coin; ~ part (for car);
  ~ n play (theater); ~ room
le pied foot
le piéton pedestrian
la pile battery
le pilier tent pole
la pilule Pill (birth control)
le piquet tent peg
la piqûre sting; ~ d'insecte
  insect bite

la **piscine** pool; ~ **intérieure** indoor pool; ~ **extérieure** outdoor pool

la **piste** trail [piste BE]; ~ **cyclable** bike route

la **pizzeria** pizzeria

la **plage** beach

la **plainte** complaint

le **plaisir** pleasure

le **plan du magasin** store directory

le **plat principal** main course

platine platinum

le **plombage** filling (tooth)

plonger v dive

la **pluie** rain

plus more; ~ **bas** lower; ~ **fort** louder; ~ **grand** larger; ~ **lent** slower; ~ **petit** smaller; ~ **tard** later; ~ **tôt** earlier; ~ **vite** faster

pluvieux rainy

le **pneu** tire [tyre BE]; ~ **crevé** flat tire [tyre BE]

la **poche** pocket

la **poêle** frying pan

le **poignet** wrist

le **point d'observation** overlook [viewpoint BE] (scenic place)

le **poison** poison

la **poitrine** chest (body part)

la **police** police

la **pompe à air** air pump

les **pompiers** fire department

le **pont** bridge

la **pop musique** pop music

le **portable** wireless/cell [mobile BE] phone

la **porte** gate (airport); ~ door; ~ **coupe-feu** fire door

le **portefeuille** wallet

la **portion** portion; ~ **enfant** children's portion

la **pose** exposure (film)

le **poste** extension (phone)

le **pot** jar

la **poterie** pottery

le **poubelle** garbage [rubbish BE]

le **poumon** lung

la **poupée** doll

pour for

pourpre purple

pousser to push (door sign)

la **poussette** stroller [pushchair BE]

précieux valuable

premier first

la **première classe** first class

prendre v pick up (something); ~ v take; ~ **plaisir** v enjoy; ~ **sa retraite** retired

près close, near; ~ **de** nearby

presbyte far- [long- BE] sighted

prescrire to prescribe

présenter v introduce

le **préservatif** condom

prévoir v schedule

la **principale attraction touristique** main attraction

la **prise électrique** electric outlet

le **prix** price

le **problème** problem

produire produce

le **produit** product; ~ **d'entretien** cleaning product; ~ **ménager** household good

profondément deeply
la promenade walk
prononcer v pronounce
propre clean
public public
le pull sweater
le pyjama pajamas

Q

le quai n track [platform BE] (train)
la qualité quality
quand when
le quartier des magasins shopping area
la question question
qui who
quitter la chambre check-out (hotel)
quoi what

R

raccourcir v mend
la rampe d'accès wheelchair ramp
le rap rap (music)
le rapport de police police report
la raquette racket (sports)
le rasoir jetable disposable razor
la réaction allergique allergic reaction
la réception reception
recevoir v receive
recharger v recharge
le réchaud camping stove

réchauffer v warm (something)
recommandation recommendation
recommander v recommend
le reçu n bill, receipt (of sale)
recycler recycling
la réduction discount
le réfrigérateur refrigerator
refuser v decline (credit card)
regarder v look
la région region
les règles period (menstrual)
les règles douloureuses menstrual cramps
le rein kidney (body part)
la relation relationship
remercier v thank
le remonte-pentes drag lift
la remorque trailer
remplir v fill out (form)
rencontrer v meet (someone)
le rendez-vous appointment
rendre v return (something)
les renseignements information (phone)
réparer v fix (repair)
le repas meal
repasser v iron
répéter v repeat
la réservation reservation
la réserve naturelle nature preserve
réserver v reserve
le résident européen EU resident
respirer v breathe
le responsable manager
le restaurant restaurant

rester v stay

retarder v delay

retirer v withdraw

le retrait withdrawal (bank);
  ~ **des bagages** baggage claim

la réunion meeting

réveiller v wake

le rez-de-chaussée ground floor

le rhume cold (sickness)

rien anything, nothing

la rivière river

la robe dress (piece of clothing)

romantique romantic

rose pink

rouge red

la route route

le Royaume Uni United Kingdom (U.K.)

le rugby rugby

les ruines ruins

le ruisseau stream

S

s'asseoir v sit

s'il vous plaît please

le sac bag, purse; ~ **à dos** backpack; ~ **à appareil photo** camera case; ~ **de couchage** sleeping bag; ~ **à main** purse [handbag BE]; ~ **poubelle** garbage [rubbish BE] bag

le sachet bag

saigner v bleed

le saladier bowl

sale dirty

la salle room:
  ~ **d'attente** waiting room;

~ **de concert** concert hall;
  ~ **à manger** dining room;
  ~ **de réunion** meeting room

le salon d'essayage fitting room

salut hi

les sandales sandals

le sang blood

sans without; ~ **0% de matières grasses** fat free; ~ **ordonnance** over the counter (medication);
  ~ **plomb** unleaded (gasoline);
  ~ **surveillance** unattended

la santé health

Santé! Cheers!

le sauna sauna

sauvegarder v save (computer)

le savon soap

le scanner scanner

la science science

le sèche-cheveux hair dryer

le secouriste lifeguard

la sécurité security

le sein breast

le self-service self-service

la semaine week

le séminaire seminar

les seniors senior citizens

le sens unique one-way street

séparé separated (marriage)

sérieux serious

la serpillière mop;
  ~ **groundcloth**

le serveur waiter

la serveuse waitress

le service service (in a restaurant);
  ~ **de chambre** room service;
  ~ **complet** full-service;
  ~ **d'entretien** housekeeping

services; ~ **internet** internet service; ~ **de nettoyage** laundry service

la serviette napkin, towel; ~ **hygiénique** sanitary napkin [pad BE]

seul alone

seulement only

le shampooing shampoo

le short shorts

le siège seat; ~ **bébé** car seat; ~ **couloir** aisle seat; ~ **enfant** child's seat

signer v sign

le silence quiet

le ski ski; ~ **jet** jet ski

skier v ski

les skis nautiques water skis

les slips briefs [underpants BE] (clothing)

le snowboard snowboard

la sœur sister

la soie silk

soif thirsty

le soin à l'oxygène oxygen treatment

le soin du visage facial

la soirée evening

le sol floor

le soleil sun

la solution pour lentilles de contact contact lens solution

sombre dark

le sommet peak

somnolence drowsiness

la serviette en papier paper towel

la sortie exit; ~ **de secours** emergency exit

sortir to exit

la source chaude hot spring

sourd deaf

les sous-vêtements underwear

le soutien-gorge bra

le souvenir souvenir

le spa spa

la spatule spatula

le spécialiste specialist (doctor)

le sport sports

le stade stadium

la station station; ~ **de métro** subway [underground BE] station; ~ **service** gas [petrol BE] station

la statue statue

stupéfiant stunning

le style de coiffure hairstyle

le stylo pen

subtil subtitle

sucré sweet (taste)

sud south

suivant next

le super super (fuel)

supérieur upper

le supermarché supermarket

la supervision supervision

supprimer v delete (computer)

le surf surfboard

surprenant amazing

le sweat-shirt sweatshirt

le symbole symbol (keyboard)

la synagogue synagogue

le syndicat d'initiative tourist information office

le Syndrome d'immunodéficience acquise (SIDA) AIDS

T

le tabac tobacconist
la table table
la taille size
le tampon tampon
frapper *v* (computer) type
le tapis de sol groundcloth
tard late (time)
la tasse cup
le taux de change exchange rate
la taxe duty (tax)
le taxi taxi
la teinturerie dry cleaner
la télé TV; ~le téléphérique
 cable car; ~le téléphone
 phone; ~le téléphone public
 pay phone
téléphoner *v* phone
le télésiège chair lift
le temple temple (religious)
temporaire temporary
le temps time, weather; ~ partiel
 part-time; ~ plein full-time
le tennis tennis
les tennis sneakers
la tension blood pressure
la tente tent
la tenue exigée dress code
le terminal terminal (airport)
terminer une session *v* log off
 (computer)
le terrain field, course; ~ de golf
 golf course
la terre cuite terracotta
terrible terrible
la tête head (body part)
la tétine pacifier [soother BE]

le texte text (message)
le théâtre theater
le ticket ticket; ~ de bus bus
 ticket
le timbre stamp (postage)
le tirage unique single prints
le tire-bouchon corkscrew
tirer *v* pull (door sign)
les toilettes restroom
 [toilet BE]
les toilettes portables
 chemical toilet
tôt early
total total (amount)
la tour tower
le touriste tourist
le tournoi de golf golf tournament
tousser *v* cough
tout de suite right of way
la toux cough
traditionnel traditional
traduire *v* translate
le train train
tranchant sharp
la tranche slice
travailler *v* work
très grand extra large
triste sad
trop too
le t-shirt T-shirt
la TVA sales tax [VAT BE]

U

un one
une fois once
l'université university
l'urgence emergency

urgent urgent
l'ustensile utensil
les produits d'entretien
  cleaning supplies
utiliser v use

V

les vacances vacation [holiday BE]
la vaccination vaccination
le vagin vagina
la vaisselle dish (kitchen)
la valeur value
valide valid
la valise suitcase
la vallée valley
végétarien vegetarian
le véliplanchiste windsurfer
le vélo tout terrain (VTT)
  mountain bike
vendre v sell
venir v come
le ventilateur fan (appliance)
vérifier v check (on something)
le verre glass, lens
vert green
la vessie bladder
la veste jacket
les vêtements clothing
le veuf widowed
vider v empty
vieux old
le vignoble vineyard
le village village
la ville town
le viol rape
violer v rape

le visage face
la visite tour; ~ en bus bus
  tour
la visite touristique sightseeing
  tour
visiter v visit
la vitamine vitamin
vite fast
la vitrine display case
vivre v live
voir v see
la voiture car; ~ automatique
  automatic car; ~ de location
  car rental [hire BE]; ~ de location
  rental [hire BE] car; ~ manuelle
  manual car
le vol flight; ~ theft; ~ national
  domestic flight; ~ international
  international flight
volé stolen
voler v rob, steal
le voleur thief
vomir v vomit
le voyage trip
vrai real

W

le wagon couchette sleeper
  [sleeping BE] car
le week-end weekend
wireless internet wireless
  internet service

Z

la zone fumeur smoking (area)
le zoo zoo

Don't let a little thing like language come between you and your dreams.

Berlitz®

Berlitz® expands your world with **audio programs, dictionaries, phrase books** and **learning tools** in **30 languages.**

A wide selection of handy **travel guides** lets you explore it.

Available at your local bookseller or www.berlitzpublishing.com